The Essential Food Storage Cookbook

Combining Food Storage with Everyday
Ingredients for Delicious Food

The Essential Food Storage Cookbook

Combining Food Storage with Everyday Ingredients for Delicious Food

By Tami Girsberger and Carol Peterson

LEATHERWOOD
PRESS

For more information on food storage,
Tami and Carol's favorite supplies, and updates
on *The Essential Food Storage Cookbook*, go to
www.essentialfoodstoragecookbook.com.

Leatherwood Press LLC
8160 South Highland Drive
Sandy, Utah 84093
www.leatherwoodpress.com

Reprinted 2008, 2009

ISBN: 978-1-59992-076-4

This book is dedicated to

Our mothers, Diane Adamson and Alice Willardson, who not only taught us the joy of cooking but have been the supreme examples of cooking delicious and healthy family meals throughout our lives.

Our husbands and children, who enthusiastically embraced and sometimes endured our recipe testing, and who increase our passion and love for good food as we teach them the joy of eating delicious and healthy family meals.

A special thank you to Shelly Delaney, Cheryl Knighton, and Kristen von Rosen, our kitchen testers, who worked tirelessly to help us perfect each recipe.

Contents

Introduction

I have learned that when you mention the words "food storage" there are three types of people. The first type is plagued with guilt. They believe in the theory of food storage and that yes, everyone should have one, or least "some." However, they personally are not actively working on obtaining a year's supply of food. They have a few extra cans in the cupboard and they may even have a case or two of #10 cans from the cannery in the basement but 1) they believe food storage is made up of foods they will never use unless, of course, there is a "real" emergency in which case they would eat anything; thus, it is hard to justify the time, the cost, and the space for food storage and 2) they don't really believe there will be a need to live on food storage in their lifetime and, if they do, their neighbors will share or perhaps they will just live with their parents.

The second type does indeed have a one-year supply of food or at least a partial year supply that they plan to increase (or not). They have purchased a package deal and checked it off their list. They have no intention of rotating it and plan to throw it away or give it to the Food Bank in 20 years. On the outside they feel good but deep down inside they hope they *never* have to use it.

The third group realizes a true need for food storage not only as a commandment but also as a need in our unstable world of terrorism and natural disasters. This group has a sincere desire to have a working food storage that is not only used and rotated but one that tastes great. They want a food storage that their family will both eat and enjoy as well as one that is healthy. They don't plan to throw it away or give it away. They plan to use it and replenish it. These people are actively engaged in a good cause.

This book will change your perspective on food storage. It will teach you what to store to meet the needs of your family. It will also teach you how to stock your pantry and freezer so that preparing family meals is not only convenient, delicious, and nutritious, but also helps you to use and rotate your food storage. It is simple. It is fun. It is easy. It is healthy. And yes, it tastes great!

Getting Started

The question I get asked the most is "Where do I start?" That's easy. You start exactly as the First Presidency has instructed us to do. In a letter dated January 20, 2002 the First Presidency encouraged members to have a year supply of basic food storage items. They wrote:

> "Church members can begin their home storage by storing the basic foods that would be required to keep them alive if they did not have anything else to eat. Depending on where members live, those basics might include water, wheat or other grains, legumes, salt, honey or sugar, powdered milk, and cooking oil. When members have stored enough of these essentials to meet the needs of their family for one year, they may decide to add other items that they are accustomed to using day to day."

More recent counsel has encouraged members to build a three-month supply.

> "Build a small supply of food that is part of your normal, daily diet. One way to do this is to purchase a few extra items each week to build a one-week supply of food. Then you can gradually increase your supply until it is sufficient for three months."

The basics (wheat and other grains, legumes, salt, honey or sugar, powdered milk, and cooking oil) are the foundation of your food storage. These "other items" or "three-month supply of food that is part of your normal, daily diet" are your pantry and freezer items. These "pantry items" used in conjunction with your food storage are what make your food storage taste great and make cooking convenient. You will use and rotate your food storage while adding vital nutrients to your diet. Cooking will be fun and easy with the ingredients right in your well-stocked pantry and food storage.

Getting the basic one-year supply of food storage may seem cumbersome and expensive. It may even be hard. However, it is also rewarding. I have often thought that food storage may not only be a physical commandment but also a spiritual commandment. We may never encounter a critical situation in our lifetime in which we solely rely upon our food storage for survival. But I believe that everyday we encounter situations where we must solely rely upon the words of our prophet and our faith. Perhaps storing food, a year's supply of food, is a test of our faith.

In the Old Testament we learn that Naaman, a Syrian, comes to Elisha to be healed of leprosy. He is instructed by the prophet to "wash in the Jordan seven times, and thy flesh shall come again to thee, and thou shalt be clean" (2 Kings 5:10). Do you really think there was anything magical or miraculous about washing seven times in the Jordan River? Apparently Naaman didn't think so either because he was "wroth, and went away" (2 Kings 5:11). If simply washing seven times in the Jordan cured leprosy, don't you think every leper in the area would be washing in the river Jordan? Washing in the Jordan seven times was a test of Naaman's faith. Later, Naaman returns and dips himself in the Jordan and is healed (2 Kings 5:14). The miracle came through faith and obedience. However, he had to fulfill the physical commandment in order to enjoy the blessing of being healed. Do you think there is anything life-saving or miraculous about storing food? Possibly. Do you think there is anything life saving or miraculous about obeying the prophet? Definitely. If we only store food out of obedience, I believe we are living a higher law. I believe we will find our reward even if we never encounter a critical situation in our lifetime where we must rely solely on our food storage for survival.

Don't let this task get overwhelming. The First Presidency also states in the same letter dated January 20, 2002 that:

"Some members do not have the money or

Suggested Amounts of Basic Foods for Home Storage

Per person for one year.
This list may vary according to location.

Grains	400 lbs.
Beans and Legumes	60 lbs.
Powdered Milk	16 lbs.
Cooking Oil	10 qts.
Sugar or Honey	60 lbs.
Salt	8 lbs.
Water (2 weeks)	14 gal.

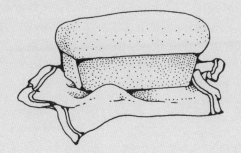

space for such storage, and some are prohibited by law from storing a year's supply of food. These members should store as much as their circumstances allow. Families who do not have the resources to acquire a year's supply can begin their storage by obtaining supplies to last for a few months."

The key is to be obedient in following this counsel and we do this by being actively engaged in obtaining a year's supply of essentials and a three-month supply of our pantry items. It doesn't mean we have to purchase it all at once. We are obedient as we strive to reach the goal of a one year's supply not only after we have achieved it. Creating a plan and by adding a few cans a month, or whatever your means allow, is being actively engaged in being obedient.

Listed in the box on the previous page are the suggested amounts of food needed for one person per year.

When you multiply these amounts by the number of people in your family, the task does indeed seem overwhelming. This is the hard part. However, these food storage items contain vital nutrients with long-term storage qualities that are absolutely essential in our diets.

I believe that if we truly incorporated the essential foods as recommended by the First Presidency into our daily diet, we would be a healthier people. Don't get caught up in eating processed foods that are quick and easy. Not only is it unhealthy but it makes the task of storing and rotating food practically insurmountable.

When these basic foods are combined with your pantry foods, not only will you be using and rotating your food storage, but you will be glad to have it and anxious to replenish what you use. You won't see cans that are taking up space that you hope you never have to open. You will see an extended pantry of food that you want to eat and that you know how to prepare. You will see nourishment for your family for an entire year. You will feel an added measure of peace and security. You will feel the accomplishment of being obedient as well as one of being prepared—and it's exhilarating!

Grains

The recommended amount of grains to store for one year is 400 lbs. per person. These 400 lbs. can be made up of any combination of grains that you like, use, and know how to prepare. The most common grains to store are wheat, oats, flour, rice, pasta, popcorn, and barley. Variety is key. Every grain has a different make-up of vitamins and nutrients. Preparing and eating many grains broadens your spectrum of these nutrients and makes for a healthier you and a healthier family.

Wheat

Wheat is an absolute must. For starters it is not expensive. It stores for long periods of time without losing nutrition and wheat is very healthy to use in our daily diet. Quality wheat can contain as much as 18% protein. That's awesome! Now, before you roll your eyes and close this book, know that although wheat is possibly the most intimidating grain, it is the easiest grain to use with a real punch of nutrition.

The two most common varieties of wheat to use and store for home use are hard white wheat and hard red wheat. The white wheat is lighter in color, texture, and taste. Red wheat produces a darker, denser and more flavorful product. If your family is not use to eating wheat, I recommend storing white wheat. An added bonus is that it is easy to substitute white wheat flour for white flour in recipes without causing an upheaval in your family. In fact, they may never know. However, the nutritional impact is phenomenal.

There is a catch. If you store wheat, you do need a wheat grinder. I only know of a handful of things to do with whole-wheat berries. However, the ability to grind wheat into flour opens up a whole new world of options. I grind wheat weekly and fill my wheat flour bin that sits in my pantry right next to my white flour bin. Anything you make—cookies, cakes, muffins, waffles, pancakes, breads, etc.—can be made with at least some whole-wheat flour. One cup white flour, one cup wheat flour.

It is extremely easy if you make it convenient. Store your wheat grinder on an "easy to reach" shelf in the kitchen and have a bucket of wheat handy. My bucket of wheat sits on the floor of my pantry and is topped with a gamma lid that is easy to twist on and off. For me, grinding wheat entails moving the grinder from its "easy to reach" shelf in the kitchen (not the garage or the storage room in the basement) to the countertop in the kitchen (several steps at the most). I then open a bucket of wheat in my pantry and fill a bowl of wheat. I pour the wheat into the grinder and turn the grinder on. Ten minutes later, I have a bin of whole-wheat flour. Easy! And the added nutrition to your diet and the diet of your family is completely beneficial.

If you are not currently using wheat, start. It is a lifestyle change that could save your life. Now here's the best part. When you go into your garage or your storage room and see buckets upon buckets of stacked wheat, you will smile. You won't be filled with dread or guilt. You will know that you plan to use those buckets of wheat one by one. You will see layers of nutrients, minerals, and vitamins that will help feed and protect your family. You will be actively engaged in a good cause.

Oats

Oats are probably the most popular whole grain. They have a universally pleasing flavor for both the old and the young and they get a lot of air time for being a "heart healthy" food—which is true. They are full of dietary fiber, which has been proven to lower cholesterol and the risk of heart disease. Oats also contain iron, thiamin, and many other vitamins.

Oats are most common as quick oats or regular oats (also known as rolled oats). Some people like to store oat groats and then make their own rolled oats with an oat roller. Some people prefer instant oats. Whatever your preference, eat more oats. And store more oats! They have a shelf life of five years and make an excellent choice for both everyday living and long-term storage.

White Flour

If your family hasn't completely converted to whole-wheat flour, you should store some white flour. Flour can be canned in #10 cans or purchased in food grade 6-gallon buckets. Either is fine, however, the #10 cans are so convenient to rotate that most people really will rotate them.

White flour is typically stored for calories and carbohydrates, not for nutritional content. I have often said that white flour starts with no nutrition and ends with no nutrition. Some manufacturers add vitamins to the flour but they do not last during storage. In other words, don't count on your white flour for nutrition. Stick to it for bulk.

If you use white flour frequently, purchase the 5 lb. bags in the fall when they go on sale. Most grocery stores will use them as a loss leader and you can get some excellent prices. I once purchased 50 bags for $.70 each! I dropped each bag, packaging and all, in a gallon-sized Ziploc bag, and set them on the shelf in my storage room. This works very well if you don't have creatures living in your storage room. If you do, stick to the cans. They are safe and convenient. I also like to purchase "Better for Bread" flour. It contains more gluten than regular flour and is used for making yeast breads.

Rice

Rice is a universal favorite and a staple worldwide. It is an important source of complex carbohydrates, fiber, and essential nutrients, and when combined with beans, it makes a complete protein—healthy now and crucial when living off your food storage in the event of an emergency.

White rice is usually enriched with vitamins which unfortunately are depleted over time. Once again, the #10 cans are most convenient, but rice also stores well when properly packaged in food grade 6-gallon buckets. My sister has an amazing food storage rotating system using almost exclusively 6-gallon buckets. It really comes down to your personal preference and what works for you. White rice stores for 8 to 10 years. *Do not* rinse rice as it washes away nutrients.

Brown rice is also an excellent storage item. However, it is *not* something that you can can yourself. Because of its oil and moisture content, brown rice needs to be canned in special anodized cans and has a shelf life of about 4 years. Brown rice is a healthier alternative to white rice and contains magnesium, oryzanol (found in the bran layer of brown rice), selenium, insoluble fiber, and substantial quantities of vitamin B6. Brown rice has a mild nutty flavor and is absolutely delicious. In fact, my family never knew I made the switch.

Pasta

Store your favorite pasta. It comes in lots of shapes and sizes. The two most popular being spaghetti and elbow macaroni. Pasta has very little nutrition and is stored mostly for the bulk of calories and carbohydrates, which are indeed important in times of emergencies. Because pasta has few to none vitamins, it can be shelf stable similar to flour without being canned, unless, of course, you have bugs of sort in your storage area! Perhaps can the spaghetti and macaroni and leave it on the shelf a little longer while you use packaged pasta that are your family favorites.

Popcorn

I love storing popcorn. It is a whole grain packed with nutrition and stores that nutrition for long periods of time. Most people immediately ask what I do with popcorn. Popcorn can be run through your wheat grinder to make cornmeal and used in a variety of baked items.

Popcorn can also be popped and made into a myriad of fun treats. One of our favorite snacks is to pop popcorn on the stove. We add a little oil, sugar, and vanilla, and call it Vanilla Glazed Popcorn. We also dust it with cinnamon and sugar for Cinnamon Crunch Popcorn. It pops in literally just minutes and makes a great snack for Family Home Evening, game night, or just for fun.

You can pop popcorn in a heavy pan with a couple of tablespoons of oil (enough to cover bottom of pan) and ½ cup of popcorn (you can also add 2 tablespoons of sugar to make kettle corn). Cover and shake pan over heat to keep the popcorn moving so it doesn't burn. Easy! I have learned that this method is quickest and easiest on a gas stovetop rather than an electric.

You can also purchase some commercial popcorn poppers like the Whirly Pop or an air popper. Pop popcorn into your diet and pop a punch of dietary fiber.

Barley

When it comes to good nutrition, barley is a winner. Barley is packed with fiber both soluble, and insoluble as well other vitamins, minerals, antioxidants, and phytochemicals that contribute to good health. Barley is best stored in anodized #10 cans and has a shelf life of about 4 years. Barley has a mild and very appealing flavor. You can run barley through your wheat grinder to make barley flour and add it to baked goods. It's a great way to add a different assortment of nutrition to your diet.

Beans and Legumes

Legumes, which include dry beans, split peas, lentils, etc., are the best plant sources of protein. They also contain dietary fiber, calcium, iron, folate, and phytochemicals. Legumes are something that should be in our diet every single day. You can hardly pick up a health magazine or read an article regarding good health without it imparting advice to eat more whole grains and legumes. Don't be afraid to use more beans. You can make it both easy and delicious. The recommended amount of legumes to store is 60 lbs. per person.

Wet-packed canned beans are excellent for the convenience factor. You can buy cases of canned beans at case lot sales at grocery stores or you can volunteer at the Church wet-pack cannery, when beans are being canned, and buy cases of beans. They are very reasonably priced. Although they are more expensive than dry beans and bulkier to store then dry beans, if it is convenience that gets beans into your diet, then store them wet-packed and ready to use. Note that wet-packed beans will have to be used and rotated more frequently than dry beans.

Dry beans are excellent because they are extremely inexpensive, they store very well and, if package properly, they can have a shelf life of over 10 years. However, using dry beans takes a little planning and forethought. Dry beans are easily canned in #10 cans or packed in food grade storage buckets. Both require oxygen absorbers. Perhaps a combination of both dry-packed and wet-packed beans in your food storage is ideal.

The most popular beans to store are black, white, pinto, red, pink, kidney, garbanzo, lima, and soybean.

Other legumes common to store are split peas, whole peas, lentils, and black-eye peas.

Bean Flour

Dry beans can be run through your wheat grinder to make bean flour. Bean flour makes a great thickener and can be used to thicken soups, sauces, and gravies. You can also add bean flour to most baked goods. Substitute 1 to 2 table-spoons of bean flour for the 1 to 2 tablespoons of white flour in recipes to add punch of nutrition to your diet. Because bean flour has no gluten, only use it to replace up to ¼ of the amount of flour called for in recipes (i.e., if recipes calls for 2 cups flour, only replace up to ½ cup bean flour).

Powdered Milk

Dehydrated milk is not often something we hope to reconstitute and drink as a substitute for our regular fluid dairy milk. However, good quality powdered milk is high in protein and calcium, low in calories, and can be great to cook with. The bonus is that by storing powdered milk you open up a whole new world of dairy products in your food storage. And, in the event that you really do one day need to live off of your food storage, the calcium is a must, especially for young growing children.

But don't wait until "something happens" to use your powdered milk. There are surprisingly, lots of fun and delicious foods to make and by using your powdered milk if you keep it rotated

Bean Math

1 lb. of dry beans = 2 cups dry beans
1 can (15 oz.) of beans = 1 ½ cups cooked beans
1 can (15 oz.) of beans = ½ cup dry beans that have been rehydrated and cooked
Beans double in volume (some beans nearly triple) when soaked and cooked.

Soaking Beans

Dried beans that are soaked before cooking have a more consistent texture and cook more evenly. Always sort beans and rinse thoroughly. Soak using the Quick Soak Method or the Overnight Soak Method (p. 156) using three cups of water for every one cup of dried beans. Discard the water that the beans have been soaked in as this removes some of the gas-producing sugars.

and fresh. Don't let your powdered milk become a space-taking, money-hogging burden. Use it! Enjoy it! And replenish it! It will be nutrition for your family and less expensive than fluid milk. Plus, you have the bonus of knowing how to use it if "something" does happen.

There are two types of dehydrated milk: *Instant Nonfat* and *Regular* (non-instant). I prefer *Instant Nonfat* powdered milk. It mixes very easily for a smooth texture when reconstituting and is an excellent option for long-term storage. Instant nonfat dehydrated milk has a shelf life of about 5 years and should be stored at room temperature or cooler. Reconstituted milk can be used in recipes just as you would use store-bought fluid milk. You can even mix the powdered milk in with the dry ingredients and then add the water to the recipe.

The recommended amount of powdered milk to store is 16 lbs. per person. That quantity will allow you one 8-ounce glass per day for a year. You may wish to store more for younger children or pregnant or nursing women.

Store powdered milk in #10 cans rather than 5-gallon food grade buckets. Once the milk is opened and exposed to the air, it loses nutrients more quickly and can also go bad or lumpy, especially if exposed to moisture. The #10 can seems to be a more manageable amount to use

within a reasonable amount of time. Also, the #10 can takes up very little room in the pantry. Use opened containers within 6 months to a year.

My favorite powdered milk is Country Cream, which can be found at our website, www.essentialfoodstoragecookbook.com.

Oil

The recommended amount of oil to store is 10 quarts per person. I believe the best two oils for storage are olive oil and canola oil.

Olive oil is extracted from crushed olives and is an excellent source of monounsaturated fat, vitamin E, as well as some important antioxidants. It makes a supreme option for food storage if stored in a cool, dark place and regularly rotated. Olive oil can be a bit pricey so purchase it in bulk at the warehouse stores. Olive oil imparts a nice but heavy flavor and is used best for savory breads, dressings, meats, and vegetables. Use olive oil over low to medium heat, never high heat.

Canola oil has the lowest saturated fat content of all commercial oils and is rather inexpensive and easy to store. Use canola oil for breakfast items, desserts, and sauces. Canola oil does not impart a strong flavor or change the flavor of baked items.

Powdered Milk Substitution

1 cup fluid milk	=	¼ cup powdered milk + 1 cup water
1 quart fluid milk	=	⅔ cup powdered milk + 1 quart water (4 cups)
1 gallon fluid milk	=	2-⅔ cups powdered milk + 1 gallon water (16 cups)

Did you know you can bottle butter to make it shelf stable? This method of storing butter is getting quite popular and frees up space in your freezer.

Bottled Butter

Warm canning jars in oven at 200°F and boil canning lids and rings. Melt butter in microwave or over low heat in a large saucepan or double boiler. Pour completely melted butter in warm canning jars ¼ inch from the top and place hot canning lid and canning ring on jar to seal. The heat will seal the lid within a few minutes. You will hear it "pop." You will be able to tell if the jar is completely sealed if the canning lid forms an indentation in the middle. If you can push the lid down and feel movement, the lid is *not* sealed. Wait a few more minutes. Melted butter naturally separates and needs to be shaken to be thoroughly combined as it solidifies.

When jars are at room temperature, place in refrigerator. Shake every 10 minutes during the solidifying process for the first hour. Once butter has completely solidified it will not separate. Place jars on storage shelf and use as needed. Refrigerate after opening. Butter has an "official" shelf life of 2 to 3 years. However, we have cases of bottled butter that is six years old and is still perfect.

1 lb. of butter fills 2 half-pint jars (with a little extra).
10 lbs. of butter fills 24 half-pint jars

Sugar

There are so many wonderful sweeteners available that not only store well but also add a variety of flavors to your food. The recommended amount is 60 lbs. per person.

White Sugar

A basic for cooking, white sugar is easy to store and has an indefinite shelf life. The only need is to protect it from bugs and moisture. Moisture will make sugar clump, although it will still be good. Pulverize clumps in a blender or use in recipes where sugar is dissolved in water. Canning sugar in #10 cans is easy and doesn't even require an oxygen absorber. It is also easily packaged in the mylar bags or food grade buckets.

Honey

Honey is a very popular sweetener and, like sugar, has indefinite storage qualities. Honey will crystallize over time but it is easily melted for continued use. Put container of crystallized honey in a sink of warm water or in a stockpot full of water on the stove over low heat.

Honey is most convenient to use in 5 lb. or 6 lb. containers and can be substituted for sugar in almost any recipe. The most price-efficient way to purchase honey is in 5-gallon buckets which totals 60 lbs. However, you have to be willing to endure the mess while transferring it to more usable containers.

If a recipe calls for 1 cup of white sugar, use ¾ cup honey and reduce the liquid by ¼ cup. Remember to never feed honey to children under the age of 2. Also, as another reference, 67 lbs. of honey equals 60 lbs. of sugar.

Brown Sugar

Brown sugar can be purchased in #10 cans. Because of its moisture content it must be canned in an anodized can and usually isn't something you can do yourself but is widely available for purchase. Brown sugar has a shelf life of 4 to 5 years. I actually have canned brown sugar that is seven years old and is still soft. You can substitute 1 cup white sugar and 1 tablespoon molasses for 1 cup brown sugar.

Powdered Sugar

Powdered sugar is white granulated sugar ground to a fine powder with some added cornstarch. Powdered sugar is best used for softer foods and frosting. It typically is not canned in #10 cans but is completely shelf stable at room temperature as long as there are no bugs or moisture.

Pure Maple Syrup

Pure maple syrup is a completely natural sweetener, unrefined, with a real punch of flavor. The taste is absolutely delightful. Store in a cool dry place for up to two years. Once opened, store in refrigerator. Pure maple syrup can be a bit pricey but a little goes a long way. Look for it at Costco or other warehouse stores for the best price.

Molasses

Molasses, also a natural and unrefined sweetener, is packed with iron and imparts a strong and unique flavor. You can purchase it by the gallon and then use to refill a cupboard sized jar. Store in a cool dry place make sure it is tightly closed.

Corn Syrup

Corn syrup is another liquid sweetener and comes in light or dark form. Traditional corn syrup is loaded with high fructose corn syrup which is under scientific review for adverse affects on our health such as diabetes, high cholesterol, and obesity. It is best to limit if not eliminate high fructose corn syrup from our diet. Check labels and ingredients carefully.

Other sugars in your food storage might include jams, jellies, powdered fruit drink mix, and flavored gelatins.

Salt

Salt is an essential part of any food storage program. It has an indefinite shelf life, is very inexpensive and absolutely necessary as a source of sodium in our diet. Salt enhances the flavor of our food and can also be used as a preservative. Many of the processed and pantry foods that we store (i.e. bouillon, canned vegetables, seasonings, soup bases, etc.) contain salt. The recommended amount of salt to store is 8 lbs. per person. Consider storing and using sea salt as it is an excellent storage option and contains many essential minerals.

A Well-Stocked Pantry

Pantry foods, the daily foods we are used to eating, is what makes our food storage taste great. Generously stock your pantry. In fact, the First Presidency recently counseled us in the new pamphlet, "All Is Safely Gathered In" to build a three-month supply of "food that is part of your normal, daily diet."

A good pantry makes cooking convenient. How often do we skip over recipes because we lack an ingredient or two? Of course, there are specialty items that we will always need to pick up at the store for particular dishes, but a well-stocked pantry is key to making delicious and nutritious home-cooked meals. When pantry foods are used in conjunction with your food storage, cooking can be fun and is much less expensive and usually healthier than dining out or purchasing pre-made foods.

Use our Pantry List as a guide to having a well-stocked pantry and then customize it for your family needs.

We hope to motivate people to be obedient to the counsel of our latter-day prophets by educating them on how to use their food storage in order to keep it rotated and fresh and to also generously stock pantry foods, including freezer items, for healthy yet delicious foods that are convenient and easy to make and encourage family meals.

Pantry List

Supplies
Cheese cloth
Candy thermometer
Meat thermometer
Parchment paper (jelly-roll pan size)
Kitchen scale
Muffin tin liners
✓ Nut and seed grinder (coffee grinder)

Spices/Seasonings
✓ Salt
✓ Pepper
✓ Garlic powder
✓ Celery salt
✓ Basil
✓ Thyme
✓ Rosemary
✓ Parsley
Dried cilantro
✓ Chili powder
✓ Crushed red pepper
Cayenne pepper
✓ Ginger
✓ Cinnamon
✓ Nutmeg

✓ Cloves
✓ Oregano
✓ Bay leaves
✓ Dry onions
✓ Paprika
✓ Onion powder
✓ Dry mustard
✓ Italian seasoning
✓ Mrs. Dash
✓ Seasoned salt
✓ Hot sauce or Tabasco sauce
✓ Dry onion soup mix
✓ Taco seasoning
✓ Chili seasoning mix
Zesty Italian dressing mix

Grains
✓ Wheat
✓ Oats (regular and quick)
✓ Cornmeal
✓ White rice
✓ Brown rice
Barley
Popcorn
Pasta
Quinoa (you are going to *love* this supergrain)

Legumes
Black beans
✓ Pinto beans
✓ Red beans
Kidney beans
✓ White beans
Garbanzo beans
Chili beans
✓ Split peas
Lentils

Sugars
✓ White granulated sugar
Powdered sugar
✓ Brown sugar
✓ Honey
✓ Maple syrup (pure)
Molasses
Karo syrup (check label for *no* high-fructose corn syrup)

Milk
✓ Dry instant non-fat milk
Shelf stable soy milk (plain and/or vanilla) or rice milk or almond milk

Shelf stable tofu
✓ Evaporated milk

Oil
✓ Canola and/or Vegetable oil
✓ Olive oil

Baking Items
White vinegar
✓ Apple cider vinegar
Balsamic vinegar
✓ Vanilla
✓ Almond extract
✓ Peppermint extract
✓ Maple flavoring
✓ Gelatin

✓ Bouillon (chicken and beef)
✓ Baking powder
✓ Baking soda
✓ Cream of tartar
✓ Cornstarch
✓ Yeast
✓ Cocoa
✓ Sweetened condensed milk
✓ Unsweetened baking chocolate
✓ Semisweet baking chocolate
✓ Raisins
Dried cranberries
✓ Chocolate chips—semisweet (easy to freeze)
✓ Nuts (easy to freeze)
Almonds (whole, raw—can slice in food processor)
Pecans
Walnuts
Pine nuts
Seeds
✓ Flaxseed
Sunflower Seeds

Pantry Foods
Diced tomatoes
✓ Tomato sauce
✓ Tomato paste
✓ Chicken broth
Chicken with rice soup
Canned fruits
Peaches

Shelf Life of Spices

As a general rule, spices last between two and three years. Dried herbs are more delicate and usually last between one and two years. Whole spices, like berries and seeds, store the longest at four to five years, but must be ground before use. Spices do not spoil or get rancid; however, they do lose potency and flavor over time. Gently shake the container and then smell the spice. If they have little smell, it's time to replace them. You can use more of the spice or herb, with care, in recipes if they have lost their strength. Spices should be stored in an airtight container in a cool, dry place. Do not store spices directly over the stove because of the extreme heat and never freeze them.

Pears
✓ Pineapple (chunks, tidbits, crushed)
✓ Mandarin oranges
Canned vegetables
✓ Corn
✓ Green beans
✓ Peas
Green chiles
Yams/Sweet potatoes
Pumpkin
✓ Mushrooms
Cream of corn
Mexican stewed tomatoes
✓ Canned tuna
Canned chicken
✓ Crumbled bacon (shelf stable until you open—Hormel has a *great* one)
Pasta sauce
Enchilada sauce
✓ Salsa
Peanut butter
Applesauce
✓ Jam or jelly (apricot, family preference)
✓ Ketchup
Barbecue sauce
✓ Soy sauce
✓ Worcestershire sauce
Sun-dried tomatoes packed in oil
Olives
Pickles
✓ Mayonnaise
✓ Yellow mustard
Dijon mustard
✓ Lemon juice
Biscuit mix (non partially-hydrogenated fat)
Dried mashed potatoes
Stuffing mix
Fruit juice (pineapple, apple, cranberry, family favorites)
Chocolate syrup
Pantry produce
✓ Potatoes
Sweet potatoes
✓ Onions
Garlic

Freezer Items

Butter
Margarine (non-partially hydrogenated)
✓ Shortening (non-partially hydrogenated)
Meats
✓ Chicken (skinless, boneless breasts)
Ground turkey and/or
✓ Ground beef
Roast
Fish
✓ Pork (chops / tenderloin)
✓ Italian sausage
Cheese
✓ Grated Parmesan
✓ Shredded mozzarella
✓ Shredded cheddar
✓ Orange juice concentrate and other family favorite juice concentrates
✓ Vegetables
Fruits
Milk (easy to freeze, takes 3 to 4 days to thaw in refrigerator)
Tortillas (flour and/or corn)
Bread
✓ Frozen hash browns, cubed

Quick Breads

Apple Spice Streusel Muffins

Nothing else makes the house smell so good.

2 cups flour
½ cup sugar
2 teaspoons baking powder
½ teaspoon baking soda
½ teaspoon salt
½ teaspoon cinnamon
¼ teaspoon nutmeg
½ cup butter, chilled, cut in chunks
1 large egg
⅔ cup milk
½ teaspoon vanilla
1 large Granny Smith apple (or other tart variety), peeled, cored, and finely chopped
¼ cup chopped walnuts or pecans
2 tablespoons sugar

Preheat oven to 425°F. In a large bowl, whisk together the flour, sugar, baking powder, baking soda, salt, cinnamon, and nutmeg. Cut in butter with a pastry blender until mixture resembles coarse crumbs. Measure ¼ cup for topping, set aside. In a medium bowl, beat egg, milk, and vanilla. Add the egg mixture to the dry ingredients. Stir just until the batter is blended, fold in the chopped apples. Divide batter among greased muffin cups or cups lined with paper liners. Add walnuts and 2 tablespoons sugar to reserved topping, and sprinkle on tops of muffins. Bake for 20 minutes. Let muffins cool in the pan for 5 minutes before removing them to a wire rack. Makes 12.

Banana Chocolate-Chip Muffins

Muffins make a great after-school snack.

2 cups whole-wheat flour
½ teaspoon baking soda
2 teaspoons baking powder
½ teaspoon salt
⅔ cup brown sugar
1½ cups mashed banana
¼ cup oil
2 large eggs, slightly beaten
1 teaspoon vanilla
½ cup chocolate chips

Preheat oven to 400°F. Combine flour, baking soda, baking powder, salt, and brown sugar in a medium bowl. In a small bowl, mix bananas (may use applesauce to make up the difference if you don't have enough bananas), oil, eggs, and vanilla. Add wet ingredients to dry ingredients and mix until just combined. Fold in chocolate chips. Fill muffin cups ¾ full and bake for 15 minutes. Makes 12.

Banana Crunch Muffins

Top these yummy muffins with your choice of toppings.

Muffins

- 2 cups all-purpose flour
- 1 cup whole-wheat flour
- ¾ cup sugar
- 2 teaspoons baking powder
- 1 teaspoon baking soda
- ½ teaspoon cinnamon
- ½ teaspoon salt
- ½ cup granola
- ½ cup chopped walnuts or pecans
- 2 eggs
- 1 cup mashed ripe bananas (about 2 medium)
- ¾ cup milk
- ½ cup vegetable oil
- 2 teaspoons vanilla

Preheat oven to 400°F. In a large bowl, combine flours, sugar, baking powder, baking soda, cinnamon, salt, granola, and walnuts. In a medium bowl, whisk eggs, bananas, milk, oil, and vanilla. Add egg mixture to the dry ingredients and stir until just combined.

Fill paper-lined cups ¾ full. If topping with granola, sprinkle on muffins before baking. Bake for 15 to 20 minutes or until a toothpick inserted into the center of muffin comes out clean. Let muffins cool in pan for 5 to 10 minutes before removing to a wire rack. If topping with glaze, spread over muffins while warm. If topping with frosting, frost when cool.

Makes 18 muffins.

Choice of Toppings

Granola

Sprinkle ½ cup granola on muffin tops before baking (about 2 teaspoons per muffin).

Maple Glaze

- 6 tablespoons powdered sugar, sifted
- 3 to 4 tablespoons maple syrup

Stir together powdered sugar and maple syrup to desired consistency. Spread over warm muffins.

Cream Cheese Frosting

- ½ cup butter, room temperature
- 4 oz. cream cheese, room temperature
- 1 ½ teaspoons vanilla
- 1 cup (or to taste) powdered sugar

Cream butter and cream cheese until smooth, scraping bowl twice. Beat in vanilla and powdered sugar to taste. Spread on cooled muffins. Store leftover muffins in refrigerator.

Maple Nut Muffins

Moist, tender and delicious with maple butter.

   1 cup whole-wheat flour
   1 cup white flour
   1 tablespoon baking powder
   ½ teaspoon salt
   1 egg, lightly beaten
   ⅔ cup pure maple syrup
   ⅓ cup butter, melted
   ½ cup milk
   ½ cup chopped walnuts, pecans, or hazelnuts

Preheat oven to 375°F. In a large bowl, combine flours, baking powder, and salt. In another bowl, combine the egg, maple syrup, butter, and milk. Stir the milk mixture into the dry ingredients just until moistened. Fold in nuts. Fill paper-lined muffin cups two-thirds full. Bake for 20 to 22 minutes or until toothpick inserted in center comes out clean. Cool slightly before removing to a wire rack. Makes 1 dozen.

Maple Butter

   ¼ cup pure maple syrup
   ½ cup butter, cubed

For maple butter, bring maple syrup to a boil in a small saucepan. Reduce heat and simmer for 2 to 3 minutes. Remove from heat and stir in butter until melted. Refrigerate until firm.

Blueberry Muffins

   1 ½ cups all-purpose flour
   ½ cup whole-wheat flour
   ½ cup granulated sugar
   ¼ cup brown sugar
   1 tablespoon baking powder
   ½ teaspoon salt
   1 cup milk
   1 egg
   ¾ teaspoon vanilla
   ½ cup butter, melted
   1 cup fresh or frozen blueberries
   brown sugar

Preheat oven to 375°F. Put paper liners in twelve muffins cups. In medium mixing bowl, combine flours, sugars, baking powder, and salt. In small mixing bowl, combine milk, egg, and vanilla. Beat until well blended. Add the milk mixture and melted butter to flour mixture and stir until combined. Gently fold in blueberries. Spoon batter into muffin cups and sprinkle tops with brown sugar. Bake 18 to 20 minutes or until muffins are golden and have risen nicely. Let cool for a few minutes before removing from pan. Makes 12.

Buttermilk Bran Muffins

A traditional favorite.

⅓ cup butter
1 cup sugar
2 eggs, slightly beaten
2 cups buttermilk
2 cups All-Bran cereal
2½ cups whole-wheat flour
2½ teaspoons baking soda
½ teaspoon salt
1 cup bran flakes cereal
1 cup boiling water

Preheat oven to 400°F. Pour boiling water over 1 cup bran flakes cereal and set aside to soak. In large mixing bowl, cream butter and sugar with eggs until fluffy. Add buttermilk and All-Bran cereal. Blend well. Stir in sifted dry ingredients and soaked bran cereal.

Fill muffin tins ⅔ full with batter. Bake at 400°F for 12 minutes. Mini muffins bake for 8 minutes.

Batter will store up to six weeks in the refrigerator in an airtight container. This recipe is great for a quick breakfast or after-school snack.

A medium-size ice cream scoop measures just the right amount of batter for each muffin cup.

Berry Oat Muffins

These muffins have great flavor from the berries and orange juice.

1½ cups flour
½ cup sugar
½ cup quick oats
¼ teaspoon baking soda
1½ teaspoon baking powder
½ teaspoon salt
1 egg, lightly beaten
½ cup orange juice (can use from concentrate)
¼ cup vegetable oil
¼ cup applesauce
½ teaspoon vanilla
½ cup blueberries (fresh or frozen)
½ cup raspberries

In a large bowl, combine the dry ingredients. In another bowl, combine the egg, orange juice, oil, applesauce, and vanilla. Stir wet ingredients into dry just until moistened. Fold in the blueberries and raspberries.

Fill greased or paper-lined muffin cups half full. Bake at 400°F for 20 minutes or until a toothpick comes out clean. Makes 12 muffins.

Pumpkin Chocolate-Chip Muffins

3 cups flour (try 2 cups wheat and 1 cup white)
2 teaspoons baking soda
2 teaspoons cinnamon
1 teaspoon salt
½ teaspoon nutmeg
½ teaspoon ground ginger
½ teaspoon ground cloves
1 cup (2 sticks) butter, room temperature
2 cups sugar
4 eggs
1 can (15 oz.) pumpkin
12 oz. semisweet chocolate chips
1 cup chopped pecans (optional)
1 cup powdered sugar
1 ½ to 2 tablespoons hot water
dash of cinnamon or nutmeg

Preheat oven to 350°F. Sift flour, baking soda, cinnamon, salt, nutmeg, ginger, and cloves together. Cream butter and sugar and add eggs and pumpkin; add to dry ingredients. Gently fold in chocolate chips and/or pecans. Bake for 22 to 25 minutes. As muffins cool, mix 1 cup powdered sugar with 1 ½ to 2 tablespoons hot water and a dash of cinnamon or nutmeg for glaze. Drizzle on cooled muffins. Makes 24.

Maple-Glazed Cinnamon Raisin Scones

Tender and sweet with a hint of spice. Delicious served warm.

1 teaspoon cinnamon
¼ cup sugar
2 cups biscuit/baking mix
⅓ cup raisins
1 egg
⅓ cup heavy cream or milk
½ teaspoon vanilla
½ cup powdered sugar, sifted
1 tablespoon maple syrup
1 tablespoon heavy cream

Preheat oven to 425°F. In a large bowl, combine cinnamon, sugar, baking mix, raisins, egg, heavy cream or milk, and vanilla until dough forms. Place dough on a greased or parchment lined cookie sheet, pat into an 8-inch circle. Score into 8 wedges without cutting all the way through. Bake for 12 minutes.

For glaze, mix together powdered sugar, maple syrup, and heavy cream until smooth. Spread glaze over warm scones.

To serve, separate scones into wedges.

Multi-Grain Baked Scones

A delicious cross between a scone and a doughnut.

1 cup whole-wheat flour
1 cup white flour
2 cups rolled oats
½ cup brown sugar
2½ teaspoons baking powder
½ teaspoon baking soda
½ teaspoon salt
½ teaspoon cinnamon
¼ teaspoon nutmeg
½ cup butter, cut up
¾ cup buttermilk
1 egg
1 teaspoon vanilla
2 tablespoons sugar
½ teaspoon cinnamon

Preheat oven to 425°F. In a food processor combine flours, oats, sugar, baking powder, baking soda, salt, cinnamon, and nutmeg. Pulse to blend. Add butter and pulse until mixture is coarse crumbs. Add buttermilk, egg, and vanilla with processor running. Pulse until dough forms. Scoop dough with a medium-sized ice cream scoop and place on a parchment lined cookie sheet; flatten slightly. Mix together sugar and cinnamon and sprinkle over scones. Bake for 15 to 17 minutes or until golden. Makes 12 scones.

Serve with Maple Butter on page 30 or your favorite flavored butter.

Strawberry Bread

Great with lunch or as a snack.

3 cups flour
2 cups sugar
1 tablespoon cinnamon
1 teaspoon baking soda
1 teaspoon salt
4 eggs, beaten
1 ¼ cups vegetable oil
½ teaspoon vanilla
2 packages (10 oz. each) frozen sliced strawberries, thawed and drained
1 cup chopped pecans

Preheat oven to 350°F. Combine flour, sugar, cinnamon, baking soda, and salt in a large bowl. Make a well in the center. Add eggs, oil, and vanilla. Stir until moistened. Mix in strawberries and pecans.

Pour into two greased and floured 9 x 5-inch loaf pans. Bake for 45 minutes to 1 hour (or until toothpick comes out clean).

Zucchini-Honey Bread

A delightful and moist sweet bread.

> 2 cups whole-wheat flour
> 1 cup all-purpose flour
> 1 teaspoon baking powder
> 1 teaspoon baking soda
> 1 teaspoon salt
> 1 tablespoon cinnamon
> 2 eggs
> 1 ½ cups sugar
> ¾ cup honey
> 1 cup vegetable oil
> 2 teaspoons vanilla
> 2 cups grated zucchini, (best if peeled first)
> 1 cup chopped pecans (optional)

Preheat oven to 350°F. Combine flours, baking powder, baking soda, salt, and cinnamon. In separate bowl combine eggs, sugar, honey, oil, and vanilla and whisk lightly. Add egg mixture to flour mixture and stir just until moistened.

Fold in zucchini and pecans, saving about ¼ cup of chopped pecans to top loaves before baking. Spoon batter into two greased and floured loaf pans. Bake for 40 minutes or until a toothpick inserted in center of loaf comes out clean. Let cool 10 minutes. Carefully run knife along edge of bread to loosen from pan. Remove from pans, and cool on wire racks.

Zucchini Gem Muffins

A great way to use up an abundant harvest.

> ¾ cup flour
> ½ cup sugar
> ¼ teaspoon baking powder
> ¼ teaspoon baking soda
> ¼ teaspoon salt
> ¼ teaspoon nutmeg
> ½ teaspoon cinnamon
> 1 egg, lightly beaten
> ⅓ cup oil
> 1 cup chopped zucchini
> ¼ cup raisins
> ¼ cup walnuts, chopped

Preheat oven to 350°F. Combine flour, sugar, baking powder, baking soda, salt, nutmeg, and cinnamon. Peel the zucchini if you think your kids might like the looks better.

Add the egg, oil, zucchini, raisins, and walnuts, stir until just combined. Fill paper lined muffin cups ⅔ full. Bake for 25 minutes or until toothpick comes out clean.

Muffins freeze well for later use. Freeze in sealed bags for up to one month.

Crazy Whole-Wheat Muffins

More like a cupcake, you'll never believe this muffin is made completely from stored foods.

- ½ cup oil
- 1 cup brown sugar
- 1 cup applesauce
- 1 teaspoon baking soda
- 1½ cups whole-wheat flour
- 1 teaspoon cinnamon

Preheat oven to 375°F. Mix ingredients together and pour into muffin tins. Bake for 20 minutes (8 minutes for mini muffins).

Scrumptious Banana Bread

Moist! Moist! Moist!

- 3 eggs
- 1 cup oil
- 2 cups sugar
- 2 cups bananas
- 3 teaspoons vanilla
- 1 teaspoon baking soda
- 1 teaspoon baking powder
- 3 cups flour (try 2 cups wheat and 1 cup white)
- 1 teaspoon salt
- ¼ teaspoon nutmeg
- 1 cup walnuts (optional)

Preheat oven to 350°F. In a large mixing bowl mix together eggs, oil, and sugar. Add mashed bananas and next six ingredients. Blend just until smooth. Stir in walnuts if desired. Pour into greased bread pans. Bake 40 to 45 minutes. Cover with foil after 25 minutes. Makes 2 loaves.

Sweet Cornbread Muffins

A delightful treat served warm with honey butter.

- 2 cups cornmeal
- 2 cups flour
- 1⅓ cups sugar
- 2 tablespoons baking powder
- 1 teaspoon salt
- ⅔ cup oil
- 6 tablespoons butter, melted
- 4 eggs
- 2½ cups milk

Preheat oven to 400°F. Combine cornmeal, flour, sugar, baking powder, and salt in large mixing bowl. In another bowl, combine oil, butter, eggs, and milk, then add wet mixture to dry ingredients and mix. Spoon batter into greased or paper-lined muffin cups, filling them ⅔ full. Bake for 15 to 20 minutes. Makes 24 muffins.

Whole-Wheat Quick Bread

Delicious with honey butter.

2 cups buttermilk, well shaken

1 egg

2 tablespoons butter or margarine, melted

3 tablespoons molasses

2 cups whole-wheat flour

2 tablespoons sugar

1 teaspoon baking powder

1 teaspoon baking soda

1 teaspoon salt

Preheat oven to 400°F. In a mixing bowl, combine buttermilk, egg, butter, and molasses. Stir in flour, sugar, baking powder, baking soda, and salt, just until moistened. Pour batter into a greased 9 x 5-inch loaf pan. Bake for 40 to 45 minutes or until toothpick inserted in center comes out clean. If browning too quickly, cover loosely with foil.

Cornbread

This moist cornbread makes the perfect companion to spicy chili or stew.

1 cup flour

¾ cup cornmeal

¼ cup sugar

2 teaspoons baking powder

½ teaspoon baking soda

½ teaspoon salt

1 cup sour cream

1 egg, lightly beaten

¼ cup milk

2 tablespoons butter, melted

Preheat oven to 425°F. In a bowl, combine dry ingredients. Add sour cream, egg, milk, and melted butter, stir just until moistened. Pour into a greased 8-inch square baking pan. Bake for 20 minutes or until a toothpick inserted in center comes out clean. Serve warm.

Food Storage

"The revelation to store food may be as essential to our temporal salvation today as boarding the ark was to the people in the days of Noah."

Ezra Taft Benson, Conference Report, *October 1973, 91.*

I have often thought about this quote and the many faithful saints who have passed on without ever having to use their food storage for an emergency. However, if we never have to fully rely on our food storage for an emergency in our lifetime, then why was the revelation given so many years in advance of the actual time of need?

I believe the answer is two-fold. First, it takes time to learn how to store food and how to accumulate a year's supply. As the years pass by, storage methods are learned and perfected. We now know the shelf life of the different foods and the best ways to store them, and, as these methods become more prevalent, the stored foods become more affordable and more accessible. Our Church has had time to build and implement dry-pack canneries allowing church members to have access to packing foods for storage. We also learn how to use these foods, how to cook with them, and how to insert them into our daily diets.

Second, as faithful Saints, by heeding our prophets in their counsel to store food, we hand down the tradition of obedience. Through our example of obedience, we make it easier for the next generation to be obedient in obtaining their food storage. For one of these generations, food storage will be "as essential to their temporal salvation as boarding the ark was in the days of Noah." We want them to be prepared! It could be our children, or our grandchildren, or it could be us! In any event, food storage can bless our lives even if there is no emergency. Families often have their own "urgencies" of job loss, disability, etc. wherein they rely on their storage for a period of time.

And in the end, obtaining our one-year supply of food is really yet another opportunity for us to not only practice being obedient but also to reap the blessings awaiting for us, even if we see no emergency in our lifetime.

Raspberry Butter

Great on muffins, biscuits, or scones.

¼ cup seedless raspberry jam
¼ cup butter, softened
dash of salt

In a bowl with an electric mixer thoroughly combine the jam, butter, and salt. Serve at room temperature. Store butter covered in the refrigerator.

Orange Marmalade Butter

Try this delicious butter on muffins, waffles, cooked carrots or baked yams.

¼ cup orange marmalade
¼ cup butter, softened
dash of salt

In a bowl with an electric mixer thoroughly combine the marmalade, butter, and salt. Serve at room temperature. Store butter covered in the refrigerator.

Yeast Breads

Whole-Wheat Bread

Irresistible hot out of the oven and a staple for the rest of the week. Makes four loaves.

6 cups *hot* water
⅔ cup oil (olive oil or canola)
⅔ cup honey
1 to 2 tablespoons Vital Wheat Gluten
½ cup powdered milk (optional)
6 cups whole-wheat flour
3 tablespoons yeast (try SAF instant yeast)
2 tablespoons salt
10 cups whole-wheat flour
butter

Mix hot water, oil, honey, Vital Wheat Gluten, powdered milk, and flour. At this point the batter should be lukewarm so it doesn't kill the yeast. Add yeast.

Gently mix to blend and then let it sit to sponge about 10 minutes. Add salt.

While stirring, gradually add additional whole-wheat flour until the dough begins to "clean" the bowl. If the dough is sticking to the sides of the bowl, continue to add flour. You can test for enough flour by gently touching dough with your finger. If dough sticks to your finger, add flour and keep kneading. When the dough barely does not stick to finger, stop adding flour.

Knead on low speed for 8 minutes. Turn dough onto an oiled surface (do not use flour). Turn dough a couple of times to coat with oil. Cut dough into quarters. I like to weigh each quarter so they are all 32 oz. (2 lbs.) each. Shape each quarter into a loaf and place in a bread pan that has been sprayed with oil. Cover and let dough rise 1 hour to 1 ½ hours. A good place for bread to rise is under the lights on your range.

Preheat oven to 350°F and bake 26 to 28 minutes or until internal temp reaches 190°F. You can gently push a meat thermometer through the side of the loaf into the middle for a temperature reading. Remove from oven and brush tops with butter. Let loaves sit 5 to 10 minutes before gently removing from pans. Cool on a wire rack.

Herb Bread

This aromatic and delectably seasoned bread is a delicious addition to any meal or a great sandwich bread.

½ cup milk
2 tablespoons sugar
1 teaspoon salt
1 tablespoon butter
1 tablespoon dried minced onion
2 ½ teaspoons yeast
½ cup warm water (about 110°F)
2 ¼ cups whole-wheat flour (or ½ wheat and

½ white flour)
½ teaspoon thyme
½ teaspoon dill
1 teaspoon dried rosemary, crushed

In a small saucepan, heat milk over medium heat until simmering. Add sugar, salt, and butter and stir until dissolved. Add dried minced onion; remove from heat and cool to lukewarm. In a large mixing, bowl dissolve yeast in the warm water (about 5 minutes). Add cooled milk mixture, flour, and herbs. Stir well (dough will be very wet) until smooth.

Cover and let rise until triple in bulk (about 45 minutes). Stir down and beat for a few minutes. Turn into a greased 9 x 5-inch bread pan and let rest for 10 minutes.

Bake at 350°F for about 1 hour or until internal temperature reaches 190°F.

Serve warm.

> The dough for a regular-size bread loaf should weigh about 32 ounces, so get yourself a good kitchen scale. A scale is also great for foods you buy in bulk. Some recipes call for amounts by weight, and a scale takes out the guess work.

French Loaf

A versatile bread with a crusty top yet soft inside.

3 cups warm water
1 tablespoon sugar
2 tablespoons yeast
1 tablespoon salt
2 tablespoons olive or vegetable oil
7 cups flour
1 egg white

In a large mixing bowl, combine warm water and sugar. Sprinkle yeast over mixture and let sit a few minutes to soften. Add salt, oil, and 4 cups of flour blending well. Add additional flour until dough pulls away from side of bowl and knead about 10 minutes. Let dough rise, then beat down dough after 10 minutes. Repeat this process five times. Turn dough onto a floured surface and divide in half. Roll out each half into an 8 x 15-inch pan. Starting from the short side, roll up to form a loaf, pinching edge to seal. Place each loaf at a diagonal with seam side down on a greased cookie sheet. Cover lightly and let rise 30 to 45 minutes. Cut three shallow gashes at a diagonal in the top of each loaf and gently brush entire surface with egg white (sprinkle with sesame seeds if desire). Bake at 375°F for 30 minutes, brushing again with egg white after 20 minutes of baking.

Bread Tips

Bread freezes very well. When loaves are completely cooled, place into bread bags and secure well with a twist tie and freeze. Freeze up to three months and thaw at room temperature (overnight or allow several hours).

Gluten: Gluten is protein that naturally occurs in wheat. Purchased wheat gluten is the natural protein derived from wheat or wheat flour and then dried. Gluten strengthens the structure of bread and helps to lighten the texture. A good, high quality wheat will not need added gluten to make good bread. However, the protein or gluten content in wheat varies from year to year with each crop depending on the altitude, moisture, weather, etc. Added gluten not only increases the protein level of your bread but also increases dough elasticity and promotes a good rise.

Bread Bowl Variation: Form dough from Whole-Wheat Bread (p. 40) into 8-oz. rounds and bake on a parchment-lined baking sheet. Rounds will bake for about 25 minutes (internal temperature should be about 190°F). Let cool on a cooling rack. To use, slice round horizontally about ¼ or less from the top. Scoop out the dough (grind into bread crumbs and freeze for later use). Fill each bread bowl with soup and serve with lid.

We typically polish off an entire loaf of Whole-Wheat Bread before it even cools. We all have our favorite toppings: butter, honey, jam, peanut butter, or sugar. Whichever they choose, they all seem to be shoveling this whole grain into their bodies. Woohoo! Some of our favorites after the bread has cooled are toast, French toast (fabulous!), tuna melts, cheese melts, cinnamon toast, and garlic toast. You can also cube the bread to make garlic croutons, or grind it into bread crumbs which freeze very well and, of course, there is nothing quite like a sandwich on homemade bread.

Crescent Dinner Rolls

On Christmas Eve, roll up a raisin in one crescent roll. Whoever gets the raisin recieves a small gift.

2 tablespoons yeast
2 cups warm water
⅓ cup sugar
⅓ cup butter
2 teaspoons salt
⅔ cup powdered milk
1 egg
5 to 6 cups bread flour
Melted butter

Mix yeast and water and let stand 5 minutes. Add sugar, butter, salt, powdered milk, egg and 2 cups of the flour. Beat together till smooth. Gradually add remaining flour till soft dough is formed. Turn onto a lightly floured surface and knead till smooth and elastic. Place in greased bowl; cover and let rise till double in bulk (about 45 minutes). Punch down and divide in half. Roll out one-half of dough into circle and brush with melted butter; cut into 12 pie-shaped pieces with pizza cutter. Starting at wide end, roll up each piece into crescent. Place on lightly greased baking sheet with point on bottom. Repeat with remainder of dough. Let raise till double and bake at 375°F for 12 to 15 minutes.

Pizza Dough

1 cup warm water
1 tablespoon yeast
1 tablespoon sugar
1 teaspoon salt
1 tablespoon olive oil
2½ cups flour

In a medium bowl combine water, yeast, and sugar and let stand for 5 minutes. Add salt, oil, and enough flour to make a stiff dough. Knead until smooth and elastic. Roll into a 15-inch pizza round. Top with desired topping and bake at 400°F for 15 to 20 minutes.

Multi-Grain Bread

Irresistible hot out of the oven.

2 cups boiling water
1 tablespoon salt
2 tablespoons butter
2 tablespoons molasses
1 cup cornmeal
1 cup oats
½ cup warm water
2 tablespoons yeast
1 cup barley flour
2 cups whole-wheat flour

In a large mixing bowl, combine boiling water, salt, butter, and molasses. Add cornmeal and oats and set aside to cool to lukewarm. Meanwhile, in a small bowl, combine lukewarm water and yeast. Let stand 10 minutes. Add yeast mixture to oat mixture. Gradually add the barley and whole-wheat flour. Add enough white flour, gradually, until dough starts to clean the bowl or until dough is not sticky.

Continue to knead until dough is smooth and elastic, about 6 to 8 minutes. Place ball of dough in a large bowl that has been sprayed with a non-stick spray. Cover with towel and let rise in a warm spot until double in bulk. This will take about 1½ hours.

Punch dough down and form into two round loaves. Place on a parchment lined baking sheet or a greased baking sheet sprinkled with additional cornmeal. Let rise for 30 minutes. Gently brush tops with beaten egg yolk and make two small gashes on top with a knife. Bake at 375°F for about 45 minutes.

> Pearl barley can be run through your wheat grinder to make barley flour. If you don't have barley, use additional wheat or white flour.

Parmesan Breadsticks

As my teenager once said, "These breadsticks are amazing!"

3 cups flour
2 tablespoons yeast
1 tablespoon sugar
1 teaspoon salt
1¼ cups warm water (110°F)
1 tablespoon olive oil
1 cup Parmesan cheese, grated
¼ teaspoon garlic powder
6 tablespoons butter, melted

In a large mixing bowl, stir together 1½ cups of the flour, yeast, sugar, and salt. Add water and oil and beat for 3 to 4 minutes with electric mixer until smooth. Stir in the Parmesan cheese and garlic and enough of the remaining flour to make a stiff dough.

Turn dough out on floured surface and knead with palms of hands for about one minute. Dough should be smooth and elastic. With floured rolling pin, roll dough out into a rectangle about ⅛ to ¼ inch thick. With pizza cutter cut dough into strips about 2-inch wide. Dip each strip in the melted butter and place on a jelly roll pan. You can nestle the strips right next to each other so they all fit on the pan. Let raise 50 minutes. Bake at 400°F for 12 minutes.

Braided Fruit and Cream Cheese Loaf

As beautiful to look at as it is delicious.

1 batch of Crescent Dinner Rolls dough (p. 43)
1 package (8 oz.) cream cheese
2 tablespoons butter, softened
½ cup sugar
2 teaspoon lemon juice
1 to 1 ¼ cups strawberry or raspberry jam (or use your favorite jam or pie filling)
2 cups powdered sugar
2 tablespoons butter, softened
1 teaspoon almond or vanilla extract
4 tablespoons milk

Make dough as directed in Dinner Crescent Rolls (this recipe makes 2 braided fruit and cream cheese loaves.) If desired, make half of the dough into rolls or cinnamon rolls and the other half into the Braided Fruit and Cream Cheese Loaf, using only half of the filling and icing ingredients.

In a small bowl, beat together cream cheese, butter, sugar, and lemon juice for cream cheese filling. In another bowl, place fruit for fruit filling.

On a lightly greased and floured surface, roll out one half of dough into an 11 x 14-inch rectangle. Spread half of the Cream Cheese Filling down the center third of the rectangle. Top the Cream Cheese Filling with the Fruit Filling.

With sharp kitchen shears, cut the dough on each side of the filling horizontally into 2-inch wide strips cutting from edge of dough to ½ inch from the filling. Fold alternating strips across filling giving the dough a braided appearance. Repeat process with other half of dough.

Carefully transfer each braided loaf to a lightly greased baking sheet, using two pancake turners to lift. Brush dough with egg white and bake at 350°F for 20 to 25 minutes or until golden brown. While cooling, mix powdered sugar, butter, almond or vanilla extract, and milk. Drizzle over bread. Top with sliced almonds if desired.

Cinnamon Rolls

Everybody's favorite.

 1 batch of Crescent Dinner Rolls dough (p. 43)
 softened butter
 brown sugar
 cinnamon
 raisins, nuts, or dried fruit (if desired)
 1 cup powdered sugar
 2 tablespoons butter
 2 to 3 tablespoons milk
 ½ teaspoon vanilla

Preheat oven to 375°F. I love the Crescent Dinner Roll dough to make cinnamon rolls. Make dough as listed above. Instead of rolling out each half into a circle, roll each half into a rectangle. Brush with softened butter and generously sprinkle with brown sugar and cinnamon. Add raisins, nuts, dried fruit, etc. Gently roll the dough jelly-roll style starting from the long side and cut into about 12 rounds. By rolling out two halves separately, you can make two different kinds of cinnamon rolls. Cut into 2-inch thick rounds and place on lightly greased baking sheet. Let raise until double (about 1 hour). Bake for 15 minutes. After baking, mix together powdered sugar, butter, milk, and vanilla in a small bowl as a glaze, if desired. Lightly brush on cooled rolls. Enjoy!

Italian Herbed Flatbread

This bread makes an excellent appetizer.

 Pizza Dough (p. 43)
 4½ teaspoons olive oil (may use oil from sun-dried tomatoes)
 2 teaspoons Italian Herbs (thyme, marjoram, rosemary, and basil mixture)
 8 to 10 sun-dried tomatoes, oil-packed, drained and chopped
 ⅓ cup feta cheese
 2 eggs

Heat oven to 400°F. Roll pizza dough into a rectangle and place in a 9 x 13-inch baking pan that has been sprayed with nonstick cooking spray. Press out dough with hands to edges and corners, making small indentations over surface of dough. Brush with 3 teaspoons of oil. Sprinkle with 1 teaspoon of the Italian Herbs and top with sun-dried tomatoes.

In medium bowl, combine cheese, eggs, remaining 1½ teaspoons oil and remaining 1 teaspoon herbs. Whisk well and pour evenly over tomatoes; carefully spread.

Bake 15 to 20 minutes or until edges are light brown. Cut into squares.

Breakfast

Instant Oatmeal Packets

Kids can use these packets to make their own whole-grain breakfast.

¾ cup rolled oats
1 ½ cups quick oats
½ cup powdered milk
½ cup sugar (white or brown)
1 teaspoon salt (scant)
½ teaspoon cinnamon

Blend dry rolled oats in a blender, pulsing until oats are powdery (not flour). In a mixing bowl, combine powdery oats and the remaining ingredients.

Put ½ cup instant oatmeal into zipper lock bags. Kids can easily make their own healthy and nutritious breakfast. For variety you can add toppings to each bag (i.e. raisins, diced dehydrated apples or other dried fruit such as peaches, pears, blueberries, etc.). Makes 6 instant oatmeal packets.

To use, combine ½ cup instant oatmeal and ⅔ cup water in microwavable bowl and microwave for 2 minutes. Stir. Add toppings if desired.

> Oats are a great way to add whole grains to your diet. Substitute oats for up to one-third of the flour called for in recipes for breads, cookies, pancakes, muffins, biscuits, and waffles.

Baked Fruity Oatmeal

Perfect with a glass of milk.

3 cups quick oats
1 cup brown sugar
2 teaspoons baking powder
1 teaspoon cinnamon
¼ teaspoon nutmeg
1 teaspoon salt
1 cup milk
2 eggs, lightly beaten
½ cup butter or margarine, melted
1 small apple, peeled and diced
¾ cup fresh or frozen blueberries

Preheat oven to 350°F. In a large bowl, combine oats, brown sugar, baking powder, cinnamon, nutmeg, and salt. In another bowl, combine milk, eggs, and butter. Stir into dry ingredients. Add apples and blueberries.

Pour batter into a greased 8-inch square baking pan. Bake for 35 to 40 minutes or until knife inserted in center comes out clean. Cut into 9 squares.

Variation

Substitute ½ cup raisins for the blueberries and add ½ cup chopped pecans (optional).

Apple Cinnamon Oatmeal

A real taste treat, especially on a cold morning.

2 cups rolled oats
3½ cups milk
¼ cup maple syrup or brown sugar
½ teaspoon cinnamon
¼ teaspoon salt
1 cup chopped peeled apples
cream or milk

Combine oats, milk, syrup or sugar, cinnamon, salt, and apples in a large saucepan. Bring to a boil. Reduce heat to low and cook for about five minutes, stirring occasionally. Drizzle with cream or milk. Serves 4

Our Favorite Oatmeal

The name says it all.

1 cup rolled oats
1¾ cups milk
⅛ teaspoon salt
2 tablespoons cream
¼ cup brown sugar
½ teaspoon cinnamon
¼ cup chopped walnuts or pecans
¼ cup your favorite dried fruit
extra cream and pure maple syrup

Combine oats, milk, and salt in a saucepan and bring to a boil. Add cream, brown sugar, cinnamon, walnuts, and dried fruit. Reduce heat to a simmer.

Cook about 3 to 5 minutes stirring occasionally until thick and creamy. Remove from heat, drizzle each serving with cream and maple syrup. Serves 2.

Great Oatmeal Toppings

Sliced bananas and mini semisweet chocolate chips
Berries sprinkled with cinnamon sugar
Diced pears, maple syrup, and cinnamon
Sliced strawberries, yogurt, and brown sugar
Favorite fruit spread and toasted slivered or sliced almonds
Cinnamon applesauce and maple syrup
Peanut butter and fruit spread
Crushed pineapple, sliced bananas, and macadamia nuts
Apple butter and chopped pecans

Chocolate Pancakes

Try topping with sliced bananas and maple syrup.

¼ cup sugar
2 eggs, lightly beaten
1 ½ cups buttermilk
3 tablespoons vegetable oil
1⅔ cups flour
2 teaspoons baking powder
1 teaspoon baking soda
½ teaspoon salt
⅓ cup cocoa powder

In a medium bowl, combine sugar, eggs, buttermilk, and oil. In a large bowl, combine flour, baking powder, baking soda, salt, and cocoa powder. Add milk mixture to flour mixture. Stir until just combined.

Heat a lightly greased griddle or nonstick skillet over medium heat. For each pancake, pour about ¼ cup batter onto griddle.

Cook until small bubbles form on top, about 1 to 2 minutes per side. Serves 4

To keep pancakes warm, preheat oven to 200°F. As pancakes come off the griddle, transfer to an ovenproof plate, cover with foil until ready to eat, up to 30 minutes.

Buttermilk Pancakes

1 cup white flour
1 cup wheat flour
2 ½ teaspoons baking powder
1 teaspoon baking soda
¾ teaspoon salt
2 tablespoons sugar
2 large eggs
2 cups buttermilk
¼ cup vegetable oil

Combine first six ingredients; stir well. Combine eggs, buttermilk, and oil in a bowl and lightly whisk. Add to flour mixture, stirring just until dry ingredients are moistened. May thin with milk to desired consistency.

Variation

Apple Nut Pancakes: Add 2 teaspoons cinnamon to batter. Pour batter on griddle and arrange a few apple slices on top of each pancake and sprinkle with chopped pecans or walnuts. Cook 1 ½ to 2 minutes and then carefully flip to cook the other side.

Top with maple syrup or try our Buttermilk Syrup, Cinnamon Syrup variation on page 57.

Pumpkin Waffles

Try doubling this batch and freezing them. Then just pop them in the toaster.

2 ½ cups flour
2 tablespoons sugar
1 tablespoon baking powder
1 teaspoon salt
1 teaspoon cinnamon
½ teaspoon ground ginger
¼ teaspoon ground nutmeg
3 eggs, separated
1 ¾ cups milk
½ cup vegetable oil
½ cup canned pumpkin

In a large bowl, combine dry ingredients. In another bowl, combine egg yolks, milk, oil, and pumpkin. Add to the dry ingredients. Mix well. Beat egg whites until stiff. Fold into batter. Pour onto a greased waffle iron. Cook until golden brown. Serves 4.

Tip: When whipping egg whites make sure the bowl and beater are clean and that there is not one drop of egg yolk in the whites. Also, if the egg whites are cold, it will take them longer to reach their maximum volume. Separate eggs while they are cold and cover the bowls with plastic wrap. Let stand until they reach room temperature before beating.

Apple Puff Pancakes

My favorite breakfast.

1 apple, cored, peeled and diced
2 tablespoons butter
1 tablespoon sugar
½ teaspoon cinnamon
3 eggs
½ cup flour
½ cup milk
½ teaspoon salt
powdered sugar

Preheat oven to 400°F. In a frying pan, sauté diced apple with butter, sugar, and cinnamon just until tender. In blender whip eggs, flour, milk, and salt on high for one full minute. Transfer hot apples to a 8 x 8-inch baking dish, lightly sprayed with non-stick cooking spray. Pour batter in over apples. Bake in oven for 15 to 18 minutes. Generously dust each serving with powdered sugar or top with your favorite syrup. Serve hot.

Pumpkin Pancakes

These pancakes taste like a slice of pumpkin pie. Try them with our honey cinnamon syrup and topped with chopped pecans.

2 cups flour
2 tablespoons brown sugar
1 tablespoon baking powder
½ teaspoon cinnamon
¼ teaspoon ground ginger
pinch of ground cloves
½ teaspoon salt
3 eggs
1¾ cups milk
½ cup canned pumpkin
¼ cup vegetable oil

In a large bowl combine dry ingredients. In a second bowl lightly beat eggs and add remaining ingredients. Stir egg mixture into flour mixture until slightly lumpy.

Heat a lightly greased nonstick skillet or griddle. Pour ¼ cup batter onto griddle. Cook pancakes 1 to 2 minutes per side. Serves 4. Serve with Honey-Cinnamon Syrup on page 57.

> Over-mixing the batter makes pancakes tough. Continue stirring only until a few lumps remain. They'll disappear once the pancakes are cooked.

Peanut Butter Pancakes

The chocolate chips make these pancakes extra special.

2 eggs, lightly beaten
½ teaspoon vanilla
½ cup chunky peanut butter
2 cups milk
2 cups flour
1 tablespoon baking powder
2 tablespoons brown sugar
¼ teaspoon salt
chocolate chips (optional)

In a bowl stir together eggs, vanilla, and peanut butter. Slowly add milk until combined. In a large bowl, combine flour, baking powder, brown sugar, and salt. Add peanut butter mixture to flour mixture. Stir until just combined. Heat a lightly greased non-stick skillet or griddle over medium heat. Cook 1 to 2 minutes per side. If using chocolate chips, sprinkle 5 or 6 over each pancake before turning. Serve with a maple syrup. Serves 4.

Fun Idea: Coat a 3- to 4-inch metal cookie cutter (riveted, not soldered—solder might melt.) with nonstick cooking spray. Preheat on griddle 2 minutes. Fill cookie cutter ⅓ full with batter. Cook until sides start to pull away from ring, 1 to 2 minutes. Lift off cutter with tongs, carefully loosening pancake from cutter. Flip and continue to cook.

Sour-Cream Coffee Cake

Everybody finds their way to the kitchen when they smell this cake baking.

    1 cup (2 sticks) butter or margarine, room tem-
      perature
    1 ½ cups sugar
    2 eggs
    1 ½ teaspoons vanilla
    2 cups flour
    1 teaspoon baking powder
    ½ teaspoon baking soda
    ½ teaspoon salt
    1 cup sour cream
    ½ cup sugar
    ¾ cup chopped walnuts or pecans
    1 ½ teaspoons cinnamon

Preheat oven to 350°F. With an electric mixer, beat butter and sugar until creamy. Add eggs and vanilla and beat at high speed until light and fluffy. With mixer at low speed, add flour, baking powder, baking soda, salt, and sour cream. Mix until just combined. In a small bowl, mix together sugar, nuts, and cinnamon for topping. Spread half of the batter in a greased 9-inch springform pan. Sprinkle with half of the topping. Carefully spread the rest of the batter on top. Sprinkle with remaining topping. Bake for 60 to 70 minutes, or until toothpick inserted in center comes out clean.

A springform pan is a round metal pan with high, straight sides encircled by metal with a spring that clamps tight. When baking is finished, you can unclamp the spring and remove the sides. To make this easier, place the pan on a bowl that is smaller in diameter than the springform. Release the sides and carefully pull down the sides of the pan. The bottom of the pan holds the finished cake and can be used for serving. The most common sizes are 8-, 9-, and 10-inch pans, with 9-inch pans being the most common.

Waffles

1 ¾ cups whole-wheat flour (may use part white flour)
1 tablespoon baking powder
½ teaspoon salt
2 eggs, separated
1 ¾ cups milk
½ cup canola oil

In a large mixing bowl stir together flour, baking powder, and salt. In a small mixing bowl beat egg yolks with a fork. Whisk in milk and oil. Add to flour mixture all at once and stir until blended. In a small bowl beat egg whites until stiff. Gently fold beaten egg whites into flour mixture. Do not over mix. Pour batter onto waffle iron that has been lightly greased and cook until golden brown. Serve hot with your favorite topping.

Variations

Chocolate Waffles: Add 3 tablespoons cocoa.

Oatmeal Buttermilk Waffles: Substitute 1 cup of oat flour for 1 cup of wheat flour and substitute 1 cup of buttermilk for 1 cup of the milk. Add ½ teaspoon cinnamon.

Yogurt Waffles: Substitute 1 cup of yogurt for 1 cup of milk.

German Pancakes

A Sunday morning tradition.

¼ cup butter (½ stick)
9 eggs
1 ½ cups flour (try ½ cup wheat flour)
1 ½ cups milk
1 teaspoon salt

Preheat oven to 400°F. Place butter in a 9 x 13-inch glass pan and put in oven while preheating to melt butter. (Be careful not to burn butter.) In blender, put in eggs, flour, milk, and salt and whip vigorously (1 to 2 full minutes). Pour batter over melted butter and bake 22 minutes. (Make sure oven is fully preheated before cooking). As it bakes it will puff up. Serve with fresh fruit and Buttermilk Syrup (p. 57).

Note: This recipe does not work well in stoneware.

Egg-Chile Casserole

This is a wonderful brunch dish.

8 eggs
1 can (12 oz.) evaporated milk
1½ cups cheddar cheese, shredded
1½ cups Monterey Jack cheese, shredded
4 tablespoons biscuit/baking mix
1 can (4 oz.) diced green chiles
1 cup chunky salsa

Preheat oven to 325°F. In a large bowl mix eggs, milk, cheeses, biscuit mix, and chiles. Pour into a greased 9 x 13-inch pan and bake for 25 to 30 minutes or until just set. Then top with spoonfuls of the chunky salsa spread over top. Return to oven for about 10 minutes. Watch carefully so it doesn't overcook. Serves 6.

Flavorful French Toast

Serve this yummy toast with warm maple syrup or honey.

3 eggs
¾ cup milk
2 tablespoons sugar
1 teaspoon cinnamon
½ teaspoon vanilla
pinch of salt

melted butter or oil, as needed
8 slices whole-wheat bread

In a bowl whisk eggs, milk, sugar, cinnamon, vanilla, and salt. Melt butter in a large nonstick skillet or on griddle. Dip sliced bread in the egg mixture and cook in the skillet, turning once, until golden brown. Serves 4.

Finger French Toast

A real kid pleaser.

¼ cup milk
2 eggs
½ teaspoon vanilla
2 tablespoons sugar
¼ teaspoon salt
½ cup strawberry jam (or favorite)
8 slices bread

Preheat griddle. Combine milk, eggs, vanilla, sugar, and salt in a bowl and set aside. Make 4 jam sandwiches. Cut crusts off. Cut each sandwich into 3 sections.

Dip sandwich slices into egg mixture, both sides.

Lightly grease griddle and cook until light brown on each side.

Makes 4 servings.

Yogurt Pancakes

Soft, tender, and delicious.

2 eggs
¼ cup sugar
1 cup white flour
1 cup whole-wheat flour
1 ½ teaspoons baking soda
1 teaspoon salt
⅓ cup oil
1 teaspoon vanilla*
1 cup water
1 cup plain yogurt

Mix wet and dry ingredients separately and then combine until blended. Cook on preheated griddle at 350°F.

*May use vanilla yogurt and omit vanilla. These pancakes are soft and delicious. They are irresistible when topped with berries and Buttermilk Syrup.

Variations

Orange Yogurt Pancakes: Replace water with orange juice or use 1 cup water with 2 tablespoons orange juice concentrate. Replace oil with ¼ cup melted butter. Serve with Buttermilk Syrup, Orange-Cinnamon Syrup (p. 57), and a dusting of cinnamon.

Ginger Butter

This wonderful spread is delicious on the pumpkin chocolate-chip muffins on page 32.

½ cup butter, at room temperature
½ teaspoon ground ginger
2 tablespoons honey

In a small bowl, stir butter, ginger, and honey until well combined. Serve at room temperature.

Store ginger butter in the refrigerator, or freezer for longer storage.

Maple Syrup

1 cup sugar
1 cup brown sugar
1 cup water
1 teaspoon maple flavoring
½ teaspoon vanilla
2 tablespoons butter

Bring sugar, brown sugar and water to a boil stirring constantly. Cook and stir for 2 to 3 minutes. Remove from heat and add maple flavoring, vanilla, and butter, stirring to combine and to melt butter.

Buttermilk Syrup

½ cup butter
1 cup sugar
⅔ cup buttermilk
1 teaspoon vanilla
½ teaspoon baking soda

Mix butter, sugar, and buttermilk together and boil 2 full minutes. Remove from heat. Add vanilla and baking soda.

Serve warm over pancakes, waffles, or French toast. Makes 2 cups of syrup

(In a pinch you can use ⅔ cup milk with 1 tablespoon vinegar and let sit for a few minutes or you can use ⅔ cup milk and 3 tablespoons buttermilk powder. The syrup may not be quite as thick but still very flavorful and delicious.)

Variations

Cinnamon Syrup: Stir in ½ teaspoon cinnamon

Orange-Cinnamon Syrup: Stir in 2 tablespoons orange juice concentrate and ½ teaspoon cinnamon.

Fourth-of-July Treat: Cut up strawberries, blueberries, and bananas and drizzle each serving with Buttermilk Syrup, then top with whipped cream.

Honey-Cinnamon Syrup

This is a great alternative to maple syrup. A wonderful topping for pancakes, french toast or waffles.

¾ cup honey
½ teaspoon cinnamon
½ cup butter or margarine
½ teaspoon vanilla

In a saucepan heat honey, cinnamon, and butter, stirring occasionally until butter is melted and syrup is hot. Remove from heat and stir in vanilla.

Creamy Maple Syrup

A lovely variation of maple syrup.

1 cup sugar
1 cup brown sugar
1 cup water
⅓ cup powdered milk
1 teaspoon maple flavoring
½ teaspoon vanilla
2 tablespoons butter

Bring sugar, brown sugar, water, and powdered milk to a boil stirring constantly. Cook and stir for 2 to 3 minutes. Remove from heat and add maple flavoring, vanilla and butter stirring to combine and to melt butter.

Crockpot

Dinner in One Pot

Perfect for a day away from home.

2 tablespoons oil
1 lb. ground turkey or beef
1 teaspoon seasoned salt
½ teaspoon garlic powder
¼ teaspoon pepper
6 medium red new potatoes, peeled and sliced
2 large carrots peeled, and sliced
½ cup white rice, uncooked
1 large onion, thinly sliced
1 can (10.75 oz.) tomato soup mixed with two
   cans of water

In a large skillet, heat oil and brown meat with seasoned salt, garlic powder, and pepper until no longer pink. Drain and set aside.

In a crockpot sprayed with cooking spray, layer half the potatoes, all the carrots, uncooked rice, beef mixture, onions, and the other half potatoes. Pour tomato soup mixture over top. Cook on low 8 hours.

Chocolate Lava Cake

Very moist and chocolaty.

1 cup brown sugar
1 cup flour
3 tablespoons cocoa powder
⅓ cup chocolate chips
2 teaspoons baking powder
½ teaspoon salt
½ cup milk
4 tablespoons butter, melted
1 tablespoon vanilla
⅔ cup sugar
¼ cup cocoa powder
1 ½ cups hot water

Spray a crockpot with cooking spray. In a bowl, combine brown sugar, flour, cocoa powder, chocolate chips, baking powder, and salt. Mix in milk, butter, and vanilla. Spread chocolate batter evenly over bottom of crockpot.

In a medium bowl, mix together the ⅔ cup sugar, and ¼ cup cocoa powder; sprinkle over chocolate batter. Pour hot water over top. Cover and cook on high 2 to 3 hours or until cake is set and edges begin to pull away from sides of pot. Serves 6.

Crockpot Baked Beans

This plan-ahead crockpot dish is a great addition to any BBQ.

2 cups small white beans
2 tablespoons dried minced onion
¼ cup brown sugar
1 cup barbecue sauce
¼ cup molasses
2 teaspoons Worcestershire sauce
1 teaspoon dry mustard

At night place beans in crockpot, cover beans by 2 to 3 inches with water. Cover and cook on low overnight.

In the morning, drain and rinse beans in a colander. Put beans back in crockpot. Add dried onion, brown sugar, barbecue sauce, molasses, Worcestershire sauce, and dry mustard. Cover and cook on low until beans are tender—about 2 to 4 hours.

Crockpot Burritos

pork roast
2 cups salsa
1 can of pinto beans

Place pork roast and salsa in crockpot. Cover and cook on low for 8 hours. During last hour add one can of pinto beans. Shred meat with a fork. Fill warm tortillas with meat mixture, roll and place seam down in a 9 x 13-inch pan or on a platter. Top with 1 cup salsa and 1 cup cheese and broil until cheese is bubbly. Serve with sour cream and guacamole. Garnish with sliced olives. (Sometimes we skip the broil step and microwave individually.)

Crockpot Enchilada Casserole

A slightly spicy Mexican casserole.

2 cans (10 oz. each) enchilada sauce
2 cans (12.5 oz. each) chicken, drained
½ teaspoon oregano
½ teaspoon cumin
1 cup sour cream
1½ cups shredded cheese (cheddar, Jack, etc.)
8 to 12 corn tortillas

Mix together sauce, chicken, oregano, cumin, and sour cream. Spray crockpot with non-stick spray. Layer in pot: sauce mixture, cheese, then 3 to 4 tortillas to cover cheese. Repeat, leaving cheese as last layer.

Cover and cook on low for 2½ hours.

Crockpot Lasagna

Expect your family to ask for seconds.

2 tablespoons oil
1 lb. ground turkey or beef
½ teaspoon garlic powder
salt and pepper to taste
¾ teaspoon basil
¼ teaspoon oregano
1 jar (28 oz.) pasta sauce
½ cup water
12 lasagna noodles, uncooked, broken in half
1 carton (15 oz.) ricotta cheese
2 cups mozzarella cheese, grated
¼ cup Parmesan cheese, grated

In a skillet, heat oil and brown meat with garlic powder, salt, and pepper until no longer pink. Drain and stir in basil and oregano. Combine pasta sauce with water, set aside. If your pasta sauce jar is less than 28 oz, add additional water or tomato sauce to make up the difference.

Spray crockpot with cooking spray. Place half of the noodles in bottom of cooker. Spread half the meat mixture over the noodles. Then layer half of sauce mixture, half of ricotta cheese, and half of mozzarella cheese over the meat. Repeat layers. Top with Parmesan cheese.

Cover and cook on low 4 to 5 hours. Do not overcook. Serves 6.

Pasta in One Pot

An Italian favorite.

1 jar (27 oz.) favorite spaghetti sauce
1 can (15 oz.) tomato sauce
½ teaspoon basil
1 lb. chicken, cooked and chopped,
   or ground beef or turkey, browned and seasoned to taste
2 cups penne pasta (try using multi-grain or whole-wheat pasta)
1 cup ricotta cheese
2 cups mozzarella cheese, grated
2 tablespoons Parmesan cheese, grated

Spray crockpot with cooking spray. Reserve 1 cup of spaghetti sauce for future use. In warm cooker stir together remaining spaghetti sauce, tomato sauce, basil, and the cooked meat.

Cook on high 2 hours or low 4 hours.

Stir in pasta. (If you have been using low heat, turn to high and wait 5 minutes before adding pasta.) Cook ½ hour.

Stir in ricotta cheese and reserved cup of spaghetti sauce. Sprinkle with the mozzarella and Parmesan cheese.

Cover and cook on high for an additional 10 minutes (or until cheese is melted).

Gardening

"We encourage you to grow all the food that you feasibly can on your own property. Berry bushes, grapevines, fruit trees—plant them if your climate is right for their growth. Grow vegetables and eat them from your own yard. Even those residing in apartments or condominiums can generally grow a little food in pots and planters. . . . Make your garden as neat and attractive as well as productive. If there are children in your home, involve them in the process with assigned responsibilities."

Spencer W. Kimball, "Family Preparedness," Ensign, *May 1976, 124.*

I am always amazed at the harvest just one plant can produce. If you haven't had the satisfaction and rewarding experience of planting a garden, then start! You don't need a large plot of land to have a garden. You can tuck vegetable plants within your own landscaping or use patio pots. You can also grow herbs in your window sill. There are few things more delicious than the taste of homegrown fruits and vegetables. Plus, fresh fruits and vegetables are rich in organic vitamins, minerals, proteins and living enzymes significantly contributing to good health. The bonus is that maintaining a garden is a great way to get outdoors. It can be good exercise and a wonderful family activity and responsibility.

Garden seeds can be packed and stored in #10 cans and in an emergency will become a vital part of your food storage.

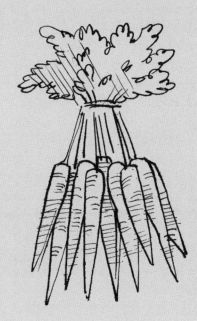

Turkey and Black Bean Soup

This is a soup my family loves. It's got a spicy, sweet flavor.

- 2 tablespoons oil
- 1 lb. ground turkey
- 1 can (14.5 oz.) diced tomatoes
- 2 cans (14.5 oz. each) chicken broth
- 1 cup carrots, thinly sliced
- 1 yellow onion, chopped
- 1 cup celery, thinly sliced
- 2 garlic cloves, minced
- 1 tablespoon sugar
- 1 teaspoon cumin
- 1½ teaspoons dried basil
- ½ teaspoon dried oregano
- ½ teaspoon chili powder
- salt and pepper to taste
- 2 cans (15 oz. each) black beans, rinsed and drained
- 1½ cups cooked rice

In a nonstick skillet, heat oil and add ground turkey. Cook until turkey is browned and no longer pink; drain. Transfer to a slow cooker. Add next twelve ingredients. Cover and cook on high for 1 hour. Reduce heat to low and cook for 4 to 5 hours. Add the beans and cooked rice; cook 1 hour longer. Serves 8

Crockpot French Dip Sandwiches

- 1 to 3 lb. beef roast
- 2 cups water
- ¼ cup soy sauce
- 1 teaspoon dried rosemary
- 1 teaspoon dried thyme
- 1 teaspoon garlic powder
- 1 teaspoon pepper
- 1 bay leaf
- 10 hoagie buns
- 10 slices Swiss cheese

In a crockpot, stir together water, soy sauce, and seasonings. Place roast in crockpot and cook on low for 8 hours (or on high for 5 hours). Remove roast from broth and thinly slice or shred with fork. Keep warm. Strain broth and skim fat. Pour broth into small cups for dipping. Slice through buns and lay open on baking tray. Line one side of each bun with a slice of Swiss cheese. Broil 2 minutes or until lightly browned and cheese is melted. Fill each sandwich with beef and cut in half on a slant. Serve hot with dipping broth.

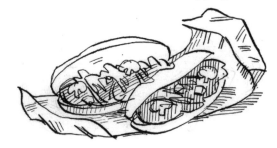

Hawaiian Pork Crockpot Dinner

A fresh, new taste to an old favorite.

  2 lbs. pork tenderloin or 4 thick, boneless pork
    chops (about 6 to 8 oz. each)
  1 can (20 oz.) crushed pineapple
  ¼ cup honey
  ¼ cup apple cider vinegar
  ⅓ cup brown sugar
  2 medium sweet potatoes

Place pork in greased crockpot. Combine crushed pineapple, honey, cider vinegar, and brown sugar. Pour over pork. Put washed, whole sweet potatoes, with skins, on top. Cover and cook on low for 10 hours. After cooking, cut up sweet potatoes and gently pull apart pork. Spoon sauce over meat and sweet potatoes to serve.

Variation

Replace pork with 4 to 5 chicken breasts.

Easy Italian Chicken

Two thumbs up for this winning chicken dish.

  5 chicken breasts, cut into chunks
  ½ cup butter, cut into chunks
  1 package Zesty Italian dressing
  1 can (10.75 oz.) cream of chicken soup
  1 package (8 oz.) cream cheese, cut into chunks

Combine chicken, butter, and Italian dressing in crockpot. Cover and cook on low for 4 to 5 hours. Then cook on high for 1 hour.

Add cream of chicken soup and cream cheese. Cook ½ hour more (add ½ cup water if it is too thick). Serve over rice or noodles. Serves 4 to 5.

Parmesan Quick Bread

A focaccia-like quick bread that goes great with soup or salad.

  1 ½ cups biscuit/baking mix
  1 egg
  1 egg white
  ½ cup milk
  1 tablespoon dried minced onion
  2 teaspoons garlic powder
  1 tablespoon sugar
  ¼ cup Parmesan cheese, grated
  ⅛ teaspoon dried parsley
  ⅛ teaspoon dried basil

Turn crockpot on to high and spray with cooking spray. In a bowl, combine biscuit/baking mix, egg, egg white, milk, dried minced onion, garlic powder, and sugar. Pour mixture into crockpot, spreading evenly. Sprinkle with Parmesan, parsley, and basil. Cover and cook on high 1 hour. Cut into 8 wedges.

Slow-Cooked Tortilla Soup

2 cans chicken *or* 4 cooked and chopped
   chicken breasts
2 cans (14 oz. each) chicken broth
2 cans (14.5 oz. each) diced tomatoes, undrained
1 can (15 oz.) black beans, rinsed and drained
1 can (15 oz.) corn, drained
1 can (16 oz.) refried beans
1 can (4 oz.) chopped green chiles
1 cup salsa
2 tablespoons dried cilantro
1 tablespoon ground cumin
1 tablespoon chili powder
½ teaspoon garlic powder

Combine all ingredients in a crockpot and cook
for 4 to 6 hours. Garnish with tortilla chips, sour
cream, and grated cheese.

Sunday Crockpot Roast
This melt-in-your-mouth roast is awesome!

3 to 4 lb. beef roast
salt and pepper
1 onion, chopped
3 tablespoons brown gravy mix
¼ cup water
¼ cup ketchup
2 teaspoons dry mustard

1 teaspoon Worcestershire sauce
⅛ teaspoon garlic powder

Place roast in crockpot and sprinkle with salt and
pepper. Add onion around roast. In a small bowl,
combine gravy mix, water, ketchup, dry mustard, worcestershire sauce, and garlic powder.
Pour over roast and onions. Cover and cook on
low 8 to 10 hours. Thicken gravy and serve over
sliced roast.

To thicken gravy, turn crockpot to high.
Transfer roast to a serving platter and cover
with foil. Add ½ cup water to juices and
onion in crockpot. Sprinkle with 2 to 3
tablespoons of flour. With the back side of
a spatula, stir vigorously, pressing out flour
lumps until thickened (about 3 minutes).

Desserts

Any-Jar-of-Fruit Cake

Use any jar or cans of fruit (peaches, pears, fruit cocktail, or a combination) in this moist, flavorful, and easy cake. Since there are no eggs, butter, or milk, this is a useful food storage recipe.

1 quart bottled fruit, with juice, or 2 cans (15 oz. each) fruit, with juice

2 cups sugar

1 cup vegetable oil

4 cups flour (2 cups whole-wheat and 2 cups white flour, if desired)

2 teaspoons cinnamon

½ teaspoon ground cloves

½ teaspoon nutmeg

4 teaspoons baking soda

1 teaspoon salt

1½ cups chocolate chips, raisins, or nuts (my favorite is a combination of all three)

½ cup brown sugar

½ cup chopped walnuts or pecans (optional)

Puree fruit in food processor or blender until smooth. Remove to a large bowl; add sugar, oil, and mix well. Add the rest of the ingredients, except brown sugar and chopped walnuts or pecans (optional). Pour into a greased 9 x 13-inch baking pan. Sprinkle with brown sugar and nuts. Bake at 350°F for 40 to 45 minutes, or until toothpick inserted in center comes out clean.

Apple Spice Cake

Granny Smith or Gala apples provide just the right tartness in this spice cake.

2 cups sugar

⅔ cup vegetable oil

1 tablespoon vanilla

2 eggs

4 cups apples, peeled, and diced

2 ½ cups whole-wheat flour

2 teaspoons cinnamon

2 teaspoons baking soda

½ teaspoon salt

1 cup chopped pecans or walnuts (optional)

Mix sugar, oil, vanilla, eggs, and apples in a large bowl. In another bowl, mix flour, cinnamon, baking soda, and salt. Add dry ingredients to apple mixture; stir well. Add nuts if desired. Pour into a greased 9 x 13-inch baking pan. Bake at 350°F for 1 hour, or until a toothpick inserted in center comes out clean. Serve with choice of toppings.

Toppings

Brown Sugar Topping

1 cup brown sugar, firmly packed

1 cup chopped pecans or walnuts

1 teaspoon cinnamon

whipped cream or vanilla ice cream

Prepare spice cake recipe and omit nuts. Pour into pan as above. Mix brown sugar, nuts, and cinnamon. Sprinkle on unbaked cake. Bake. Serve with whipped cream or ice cream.

Vanilla Butter Sauce
1 cup brown sugar, firmly packed
½ cup heavy cream
½ cup butter
1 tablespoon vanilla

In a saucepan over medium heat combine sugar, cream, and butter; bring to a boil. Reduce heat and simmer 7 to 9 minutes or until slightly thickened. Remove from heat and stir in vanilla. Serve warm with cake.

Cream Cheese Frosting
1 package (8 oz.) cream cheese, room temperature
½ cup butter or margarine, room temperature
1 ½ teaspoons vanilla
2 cups powdered sugar, sifted

Beat cream cheese and butter with an electric mixer until creamy. Add vanilla and powdered sugar; beat until smooth. Spread on cooled cake.

Favorite Chocolate-Chip Cookies
An absolute favorite with a dose of whole grains.

1 cup butter, room temperature
¾ cup sugar
1 cup brown sugar
2 eggs
1 teaspoon vanilla
3 cups whole-wheat flour
¾ teaspoon salt
¾ teaspoon baking soda
¾ cup rolled oats
2 cups chocolate chips

Cream together butter, sugar, and brown sugar. Add eggs and vanilla. In a separate bowl, mix together flour, salt, and baking soda. Add dry ingredients to creamed mixture and beat for 3 to 4 minutes. Add rolled oats and chocolate chips. Stir to combine. Drop by spoonfuls onto baking sheet lined with parchment paper. Bake at 350 for 12 minutes. Watch to make sure they don't overcook.

Applesauce Cake

Top cake with caramel sauce or orange-lemon icing. Superb.

1 cup whole-wheat flour
1 cup all-purpose flour
1 teaspoon baking soda
1 ½ teaspoons baking powder
1 teaspoon salt
2 teaspoons cinnamon
½ teaspoon ground cloves
¼ teaspoon nutmeg
1 teaspoon vanilla
1 cup honey
1 cup vegetable oil
2 eggs, lightly beaten
2 cups applesauce, smooth or chunky
1 cup chopped walnuts or pecans (optional)

Combine first eight ingredients in a large bowl. Add vanilla, honey, oil, and eggs. Mix until smooth. Stir in applesauce and nuts (if desired).

Pour cake batter into a greased 9 x 13-inch baking dish. Bake at 350°F for 35 minutes or until toothpick inserted in center comes out clean.

Toppings

Caramel Sauce

½ cup butter
2 tablespoons cream
1 cup brown sugar
1 teaspoon vanilla
¼ to ½ cup powdered sugar, sifted

In saucepan over low heat, combine butter, cream, and brown sugar. Cook, stirring occasionally, until butter melts and sugar is dissolved. Remove from heat and add vanilla and powdered sugar. Stir until mixture is smooth and becomes the consistency of a sauce. Serve with cooled cake.

Orange-Lemon Icing

1 cup powdered sugar, sifted
1 ½ tablespoons orange juice
1 ½ tablespoons lemon juice
¼ teaspoon cinnamon

Stir together ingredients until smooth. Drizzle over cooled cake.

Best Ever Carrot Cake

Next to cheesecake, carrot cake is my favorite dessert, and this is a guaranteed favorite. It's super moist and luscious.

3 eggs
½ cup vegetable oil
1 cup applesauce
2 cups sugar
2 teaspoons vanilla
1 cup whole-wheat flour
1 cup all-purpose flour
1 teaspoon baking soda
1 teaspoon salt
2 teaspoons cinnamon
2 cups grated carrots
1 cup chopped walnuts or pecans
½ cup shredded coconut (optional)

Buttermilk Glaze

½ cup buttermilk
½ cup butter or margarine
1 tablespoon corn syrup
1 cup sugar
½ teaspoon baking soda
½ teaspoon vanilla

Cream Cheese Frosting

1 package (8 oz.) cream cheese, room temperature
½ cup butter or margarine, room temperature

1 ½ teaspoons vanilla
2 cups powdered sugar

Combine and mix well in a large bowl eggs, oil, applesauce, sugar, and vanilla. Add flours, baking soda, salt, and cinnamon; stir well. Add carrots, walnuts, and coconut (optional). Mix well. Pour batter into a greased 9 x 13-inch baking pan. Bake 350°F for 45 to 50 minutes or until a toothpick inserted in center comes out clean.

Shortly before cake is done, make Buttermilk Glaze. Place buttermilk, butter, corn syrup, sugar, and baking soda in a saucepan; bring to a boil. Boil for 4 minutes stirring constantly. Remove from heat, add vanilla; mix well. Drizzle Buttermilk Glaze over hot cake.

For Cream Cheese Frosting, beat cream cheese and butter with an electric mixer until creamy, scraping down sides twice. Add vanilla and powdered sugar; beat until smooth. Spread Cream Cheese Frosting on cooled cake, over Buttermilk Glaze.

Serves 12.

Blonde Texas Sheet Cake

Moist and delicious.

½ cup butter
½ cup milk
1 ½ cups sugar
2 eggs, beaten
1 cup sour cream
1 cup white flour
1 cup wheat flour
1 teaspoon salt
1 teaspoon baking powder
¼ teaspoon baking soda
½ teaspoon almond extract
½ teaspoon vanilla

Frosting

½ cup butter
1 cup brown sugar
⅓ cup buttermilk
2 cups powdered sugar, sifted
½ teaspoon vanilla
¼ teaspoon almond extract
1 cup pecans, chopped (optional)

In small saucepan, melt together butter and milk. Set aside. In large mixing bowl, cream together sugar and eggs. Add sour cream. Combine dry ingredients in medium mixing bowl and then stir dry ingredients into sugar mixture. Add butter and milk mixture and vanilla and almond extracts as well. Mix well. Pour into a lightly greased jelly roll pan and bake at 375°F for 15 to 20 minutes or until lightly golden brown. Frost when cool.

For frosting, bring butter and brown sugar to a boil for 2 minutes, whisking continuously. Remove from heat and add buttermilk. Return to heat and bring to a boil. Pour into medium bowl and gradually add powdered sugar, vanilla, and almond extract. Beat well until smooth and creamy. Stir in pecans (optional) and spread on cooled cake.

Butterscotch Pudding

¼ cup brown sugar
2 tablespoons cornstarch
6 tablespoons powdered milk
⅛ teaspoon salt
1 ½ cups water
1 teaspoon vanilla
2 tablespoons butter
1 teaspoon molasses

Whisk brown sugar, cornstarch, powdered milk, and salt in a heavy saucepan. Add water and stir over medium heat until thick, stirring constantly. Cook and stir for 1 to 2 minutes. Remove from heat. Add vanilla, butter, and molasses. Serve warm or pour into bowl and press with plastic wrap and refrigerate. Makes 4 servings.

Caramel Sauce

½ cup butter
2 cups brown sugar
1 cup corn syrup
1 can (14 oz.) sweetened condensed milk
1 teaspoon vanilla

Melt butter in saucepan over low heat. Add brown sugar and corn syrup and mix well. Add sweetened condensed milk. Simmer 10 to 15 minutes, stirring frequently until sugar is completely dissolved. Remove from and heat and add vanilla.

Fun Idea

Make an ice cream sundae bar using cut up apples instead of ice cream. My favorite sundae toppings are Fuji apples, fresh pears, and bananas drizzled with caramel and topped with chopped Skor Bar. It makes for a fun dessert or family home evening treat that is a little lighter and healthier than using ice cream. And for those who are trying to cut back on the sugar, there is always the option of a fresh fruit cup without the extras.

Easy Frozen Yogurt
As good as ice cream, but healthier.

⅓ to ½ cup pure maple syrup
2 cups vanilla or plain yogurt
1 cup frozen raspberries or sliced strawberries

Combine maple syrup and yogurt. Place yogurt in an ice cream maker according to manufacturer's directions. With the machine running, add the raspberries or strawberries; churn the mixture until it freezes, about 20 minutes. Serve immediately.

Chocolate Dream Mousse
One bite sends you to chocolate paradise.

⅔ cup chocolate-hazlenut spread (Nutella)
¼ cup sour cream
⅔ cup heavy cream
2 tablespoons powdered sugar
1 teaspoon vanilla

Mix chocolate-hazelnut spread and sour cream in a medium bowl until smooth. In another bowl, using an electric mixer, beat heavy cream, powdered sugar, and vanilla until firm peaks form. Gently fold the whipped cream mixture into the chocolate-hazelnut mixture until thoroughly mixed. Spoon into dessert dishes or parfait cups and chill.

Chocolate Lover's Brownies

No need to use a mix when you can make these easy, delicious, and chocolaty brownies.

¾ cup cocoa powder

1 cup vegetable oil

4 eggs

1 cup brown sugar

1 cup white sugar

2 teaspoons vanilla

1 ½ cups flour (you can use ½ whole wheat, ½ white flour)

1 ½ teaspoons salt

1 teaspoon baking powder

1 ½ cups semisweet chocolate chips

½ cup chopped walnuts or pecans (optional)

Preheat oven to 350°F. In a large bowl, combine cocoa, oil, eggs, brown sugar, white sugar, and vanilla until well blended. Add flour, salt, and baking powder. Fold in chocolate chips and nuts if using. Pour into a greased 9 x 13-inch baking dish. Bake until toothpick inserted in center comes out clean, about 30 to 35 minutes.

Variation

Pinto Bean Brownies: *These fared extremely well in our taste test. You'll be pleasantly surprised!* Puree one can of pinto beans (drained well) in blender with 2 tablespoons milk. Puree very well and *make sure* there are no lumps. Stir into brownie batter before pouring into 9 x 13-inch pan. You do not need to take anything out of the original recipe. Just put in the beans. Try using all whole-wheat flour too. Surprisingly spectacular!

Chocolate Crazy Cake

Imagine a cake without eggs, butter, or milk—crazy isn't it? It's a winner.

3 cups flour

2 cups sugar

½ cup cocoa powder

2 teaspoons baking soda

½ teaspoon baking powder

1 teaspoon salt

1 tablespoon vanilla

¾ cup vegetable oil

2 tablespoons vinegar

2 cups water

Chocolate Crazy Frosting

½ cup butter or margarine, room temperature

⅔ cup cocoa powder, sifted

3 cups powdered sugar, sifted

4 to 6 tablespoons milk

2 teaspoons vanilla

Preheat oven to 350°F. Combine dry ingredients. Add vanilla, oil, vinegar, and water and mix thoroughly. Pour into a greased 9 x 13-inch baking pan and bake for 30 to 35 minutes, or until no fingerprint remains when center is lightly touched. Cool. Dust with powdered sugar or frost with Chocolate Crazy Frosting.

For frosting, in a bowl with an electric mixer, whip butter until creamy. Add cocoa, 2 cups of powdered sugar, 4 tablespoons of milk, and vanilla. Slowly mix increasing speed to prevent powdered sugar from spilling out. Beat until creamy. Add reserved powdered sugar and milk to desired spreadable consistency. Beat until light and creamy (about 2 minutes).

Note: Our favorite combination is to use 2 cups whole-wheat flour and 1 cup all-purpose flour. Try your own combo (some whole wheat, oat, barley, or rice flour) and find your favorite.

> Impressing Company? Use a vegetable peeler to make chocolate curls or shavings from a chocolate bar to top frosting. It is an awesome touch.

Chocolate Pudding

Better than boxed any day.

½ cup sugar
⅓ cup cocoa powder
2 tablespoons cornstarch
6 tablespoons powdered milk
¼ teaspoon (scant) salt
2 cups water
1 teaspoon vanilla

Mix sugar, cocoa, cornstarch, powdered milk, and salt in a heavy saucepan. Add water and stir over medium heat until thick stirring constantly. Cook and stir for 1 to 2 minutes. Remove from heat. Add vanilla. Serve warm or pour into bowl and press with plastic wrap and refrigerate. Makes 4 servings.

Our favorite thing to do with chocolate pudding? Ladle it hot over vanilla ice cream and top with chopped Skor Bar. Delicious!

Variation

Chocolate Peanut Butter Pudding: Add ⅓ cup peanut butter after pudding is thickened. Stir until peanut butter is completely combined with pudding. Remove from heat and add vanilla.

Classic Chocolate Mousse

1 envelope unflavored gelatin
2 tablespoons cold water
¼ cup boiling water
1 cup sugar
½ cup cocoa powder
2 cups cold whipping cream
2 teaspoons vanilla extract

Sprinkle gelatin over cold water in small bowl; let stand 2 minutes to soften. Add boiling water; stir until gelatin is completely dissolved and mixture is clear. Cool slightly.

Mix sugar and cocoa in large bowl; add whipping cream and vanilla. Beat on medium speed, scraping bottom of bowl occasionally, until mixture is stiff. Pour in gelatin mixture; beat until will blended. Spoon into dessert dishes. Refrigerate at least 30 minutes before serving. Top with whipping cream and grated chocolate or dust with cocoa powder. Makes 8 servings.

French Yogurt Lemon Cake

A delicious lemony cake, the glaze makes it so good.

1 ½ cups all-purpose flour
1 cup sugar
2 ½ teaspoons baking powder
½ teaspoon salt
½ cup plain yogurt
3 eggs
½ cup vegetable oil
1 teaspoon vanilla
2 tablespoons lemon juice
1 teaspoon grated lemon zest (outer yellow peel, finely grated)

Lemon Glaze

1 cup powdered sugar, sifted
2 to 3 tablespoons lemon juice

Preheat oven to 350°F. Combine all ingredients in a bowl. Pour into a greased and floured 9-inch round cake pan. Bake for 35 minutes, or until a toothpick inserted in center comes out clean. Let cake cool in pan 10 minutes. Carefully remove to a wire rack.

For glaze, beat powdered sugar and lemon juice (to desired consistency) until smooth. While cake is still warm, pour glaze over cake. Cool.

Creamy Rice Pudding

A creamy, comfort-food favorite.

2 tablespoons cornstarch
⅓ cup sugar
¼ teaspoon salt
2 cups milk (low fat or whole)
2 egg yolks, lightly beaten
1 tablespoon canola oil *or* 2 tablespoons butter,
  softened
2 cups cooked white or brown rice
2 teaspoons vanilla
½ teaspoon cinnamon
¼ teaspoon nutmeg
1 cup raisins
2 teaspoons lemon peel, grated *or* orange peel,
  grated

In a saucepan combine cornstarch, sugar, and salt. In another bowl whisk milk and egg yolks together and slowly whisk into sugar mixture. Bring to a boil over medium heat, stirring constantly. Boil one minute or until thickened, stirring frequently. Remove from heat and add rice, oil or butter, vanilla, cinnamon, nutmeg, raisins, and lemon peel (optional). Serve warm or chilled.

Ginger Crinkles

Flavorful and addicting.

½ cup butter
1 cup sugar
1 egg
¼ cup molasses
1 cup wheat flour
1 cup white flour
1 tablespoon ground ginger
2 teaspoons baking soda
1 teaspoon cinnamon
½ teaspoon salt
sugar

Preheat oven to 350°F. In mixing bowl, beat butter. Add sugar and beat until mixture is creamed. Beat in egg and molasses. In separate bowl, combine flours, ginger, baking soda, cinnamon, and salt. Gradually add to creamed mixture and blend thoroughly. Roll dough into 1-inch balls and then roll in granulated sugar. Place on a parchment-paper lined or ungreased baking sheet and bake for 8 to 10 minutes. Cookies will appear to be slightly underbaked. Let cool on baking sheet for 5 minutes before transferring to cooling rack. Makes 2½ to 3 dozen cookies.

Crazy Chocolate Brownies

Rich and irresistible. One bite sends you to chocolate paradise.

½ cup cocoa powder
2 cups sugar
2 cups flour
1 teaspoon baking powder
¼ teaspoon salt
1½ teaspoons vanilla
1 cup vegetable oil
1 cup water
1½ cups semisweet chocolate chips

Preheat oven to 350°F. In a large bowl, stir first five ingredients. Add vanilla, oil, and water. Mix well. Stir in chocolate chips. Pour into a greased 9 x 13-inch baking pan. Bake for 30 minutes.

Hot Chocolate Sauce

1 can (14 oz.) sweetened condensed milk
2 oz. semisweet chocolate
1 oz. unsweetened chocolate
1 tablespoon vanilla

Cook and stir in double boiler until thick and gravy like. Add about ¼ cup of hot water from boiler and stir until smooth.

Lemon Oat Bites

These refreshing lemon bars give chocolate treats a run for their money.

1 cup rolled oats
1½ cups flour
½ cup brown sugar, firmly packed
½ cup white sugar
¼ teaspoon salt
¼ teaspoon cinnamon
10 tablespoons butter, cold, cut into chunks
1 can (14 oz.) sweetened condensed milk
½ cup lemon juice
2 teaspoons lemon zest (outer yellow peel, finely grated), optional

Preheat oven to 350°F. Mix oats, flour, sugars, salt, and cinnamon in a bowl. Cut in butter with a pastry blender until coarse crumbs. In a greased 9-inch square baking pan, press 3 cups mixture; set aside remaining mixture for topping. Bake for 12 minutes.

Combine milk, lemon juice, and zest in a small bowl. Pour over crust and evenly sprinkle reserved oat mixture. Bake an additional 25 to 28 minutes or until lightly brown. Cool on wire rack. Cut into small squares.

Oatmeal Cake

A moist cake with a chewy, crunchy topping.

1 ¼ cups boiling water
1 cup quick oats
¼ cup butter
1 cup sugar
1 cup brown sugar
2 eggs
1 ½ teaspoons vanilla
1 ⅓ cups flour
1 teaspoon baking soda
½ teaspoon salt
1 teaspoon cinnamon
½ teaspoon nutmeg

Brown sugar topping

½ cup butter or margarine
½ cup milk
1 cup brown sugar
1 cup shredded coconut
1 cup chopped walnuts or pecans

Preheat oven to 350°F. Pour water over oats; add butter and let stand covered for 20 minutes. Stir in sugars, eggs, and vanilla. Add flour, baking soda, salt, cinnamon, and nutmeg. Pour into a greased 9 x 13-inch baking pan. Bake for 45 minutes or until toothpick inserted in center comes out clean.

For topping, in a large saucepan over medium heat combine topping ingredients. Bring to a boil. Cook mixture 1 minute, stirring frequently until butter is melted and topping is hot. Spread over hot cake.

Molasses Cake

Extremely easy to make.

1 cup whole-wheat flour
1 ½ cups all-purpose flour
½ teaspoon salt
1 ½ teaspoons baking soda
1 ½ teaspoons cinnamon
¼ teaspoon ground cloves
¼ teaspoon ground ginger
¼ teaspoon ground allspice
1 teaspoon vanilla
½ cup vegetable oil
¾ cup molasses
½ cup boiling water

Preheat oven to 375°F. Combine dry ingredients in a large bowl; add vanilla, oil, molasses, and boiling water. Mix well. Pour into a greased 8-inch square pan. Bake for 20 to 25 minutes, or until toothpick inserted in center comes out clean.

Mini Peanut Butter Cheesecakes

These are so-o-o good. You can't just eat one.

Crust

1⅓ cups chocolate wafer crumbs
4 tablespoons sugar
¼ cup (½ stick) butter, melted
16 mini peanut butter cups

Filling

2 packages (8 oz. each) cream cheese, room
  temperature
1 cup sugar
2 tablespoons flour
1 teaspoon vanilla
¼ cup creamy peanut butter (do not use old
  fashioned)
2 tablespoons whipping cream
2 eggs

Topping

1 cup sour cream
¼ cup sugar
½ teaspoon vanilla

Preheat oven to 350°F. Place a paper liner in each cup of a standard muffin pan.

To make crust, in a bowl, combine chocolate wafer crumbs, sugar, and melted butter until crumbs are moistened. Press crust into bottom of each muffin cup. Put 1 peanut butter cup into the center of each crust.

Beat cream cheese with electric mixer until fluffy, scraping down sides twice. Add sugar, beating well. Add flour, vanilla, peanut butter, and whipping cream; beat well. Add eggs, beat only until just combined. Spoon cream cheese mixture evenly over peanut butter cups. Bake until just set, about 20 minutes. While the cheesecakes are baking, combine topping ingredients in a small bowl. Carefully spoon topping over cooked mini cheesecakes. Return to oven and bake 5 minutes. Allow to cool completely. Cover and refrigerate overnight.

Makes 16 mini cheesecakes.

Variation

Mini Chocolate-Chip Cookie-Dough Cheesecakes: In a mixing bowl, beat ¼ cup butter or margarine, ¼ cup brown sugar, and ¼ cup white sugar until fluffy. Add 1 teaspoon vanilla, 1 tablespoon water, and ½ cup flour. Beat on low until combined. Fold in 1 cup mini chocolate chips. Omit peanut butter cups and peanut butter in filling. Drop a heaping teaspoon of cookie dough on crusts, top with filling, and proceed with recipe as written.

Chewy Oatmeal Cookies

A chewy cookie chock full of goodies.

1 cup brown sugar
1 cup honey
1 cup butter or shortening, room temperature
2 cups rolled oats
1 ½ cups whole-wheat flour
1 cup all-purpose flour
2 teaspoons baking powder
1 teaspoon baking soda
1 teaspoon cinnamon
½ teaspoon nutmeg
¼ teaspoon ground ginger
½ teaspoon salt
2 cups semisweet chocolate chips
1 cup raisins
½ cup walnuts or pecans (optional)

Preheat oven to 350°F. Mix sugar, honey, and butter together until creamy. Add rest of ingredients. Mix well. Drop by rounded tablespoon 2 inches apart on greased or parchment lined cookie sheet. Bake for about 15 minutes or until just set. Remove cookies to wire rack.

Old Fashioned Fruit Crisp

A favorite dessert for all seasons.

1 ¼ lbs. apples, peeled, cored, and sliced
   (about 5 medium apples)
1 cup rolled oats
½ cup whole-wheat flour
¾ cup brown sugar, firmly packed
¼ teaspoon salt
1 teaspoon cinnamon
¼ teaspoon allspice
½ cup chopped pecans or walnuts
½ cup butter or margarine

Place sliced apples in a greased 9-inch square baking dish. Set aside.

In a large bowl, combine oats, flour, brown sugar, salt, cinnamon, allspice, and nuts. In a saucepan over low heat, melt butter. Add to oat mixture. Mix well. Sprinkle topping over sliced apples. Bake at 400°F for 25 minutes or until fruit is soft and top is golden. Serves 6.

Variation

Try different fruit combinations. Our family's favorite is half pears and half apples. Peaches also make a great fruit crisp.

Pumpkin Snack Cake

Just as good as it sounds.

½ cup butter or margarine, room temperature
1 cup sugar
½ cup brown sugar
1 can (15 oz.) pumpkin
3 eggs
1 ¼ cups rolled oats
1 cup whole-wheat flour
1 cup all-purpose flour
1 tablespoon baking powder
½ teaspoon salt
2 teaspoons cinnamon
1 teaspoon ground ginger
¼ teaspoon nutmeg
¼ teaspoon ground cloves

Topping

4 tablespoons butter, melted
½ cup whole-wheat flour
⅓ cup rolled oats
½ cup sugar
½ teaspoon cinnamon

Preheat oven to 350°F. Cream butter and sugars in a large bowl with an electric mixer until light and fluffy. Add pumpkin and eggs; mix well. In another bowl, mix oats, flours, baking powder, salt, cinnamon, ginger, nutmeg, and cloves. Stir dry ingredients into pumpkin mixture until combined. Spread into a greased 9-inch or 7 x 11-inch baking pan (note: an 8-inch baking pan is too small for this recipe.)

Stir topping ingredients together in a small bowl until thoroughly mixed. Sprinkle on top of cake. Bake for 45 to 50 minutes or until toothpick inserted in center comes out clean.

No-Bake Saucepan Cookies

A fun treat.

3 tablespoons cocoa powder
2 cups sugar
½ cup butter or margarine
½ cup milk
½ cup peanut butter
1 teaspoon vanilla
4 cups quick oats
½ cup peanuts, chopped

In a saucepan, stir cocoa and sugar until no lumps remain. Add butter and milk over medium-high heat. Bring to a boil. Cook, stirring constantly, for one minute. Remove from heat. Immediately stir in peanut butter and vanilla. Stir until smooth. Add oats and peanuts. Mix well. Spoon by rounded tablespoons onto a cookie sheet lined with parchment paper or aluminum foil. Cool before serving.

Peanut Butter Cookies

Easy to make and they disappear fast.

- 1 cup butter, margarine, or shortening at room temperature
- 1 cup peanut butter
- 1 cup sugar
- 1 cup brown sugar
- 1 ½ teaspoons vanilla
- 2 eggs
- 1 ½ cups whole-wheat flour
- 1 cup all-purpose flour
- 1 teaspoon baking powder
- 1 ½ teaspoons baking soda
- ½ teaspoon salt
- ¾ cup chopped peanuts (optional)
- ⅓ cup sugar for rolling

Preheat oven to 350°F. Cream together butter, peanut butter, and sugars in a large bowl. Stir in vanilla and eggs one at a time until mixture is light and fluffy. Reduce speed to low, add dry ingredients, and beat until incorporated.

Form dough into half-inch balls. Roll in sugar and place on ungreased or parchment paper-lined baking sheet, 2 inches apart. Gently flatten cookies with back of fork to form a crisscross pattern. Bake for 12 to 15 minutes. Cool 2 minutes on baking sheet. Remove to wire rack.

Peanut Butter Chocolate Drops

A sweet treat that uses no eggs or fresh milk.

- 1 cup flour
- ½ teaspoon baking powder
- ½ teaspoon baking soda
- ½ teaspoon salt
- ⅔ cup sweetened condensed milk
- ⅓ cup chunky or creamy peanut butter (not old fashioned style)
- 1 teaspoon vanilla
- ½ cup semisweet chocolate chips
- ⅓ cup chopped peanuts (optional)

Preheat oven to 375°F. In a bowl, combine flour, baking powder, baking soda, and salt. Set aside. In large bowl, beat sweetened condensed milk, peanut butter, and vanilla. Add dry ingredients to milk mixture until completely blended. Fold in chocolate chips and peanuts if desired.

Using a tablespoon, measure dough, shape into balls, and place 2 inches apart on an ungreased cookie sheet. Bake for 10 to 12 minutes. Cool 2 to 3 minutes before removing to wire racks.

Makes 18 drops.

Pinto Bean Spice Bundt Cake

Wonderful!

1 cup butter, room temperature
1 cup white sugar
½ cup brown sugar, firmly packed
2 teaspoons vanilla
2 eggs
⅔ cup milk
1⅔ cups cooked pinto beans, mashed or pureed (may use canned pinto beans)
1 cup whole-wheat flour
1 cup all-purpose flour
1 teaspoon baking soda
1½ teaspoons baking powder
2 teaspoons cinnamon
¼ teaspoon nutmeg
¼ teaspoon ground cloves
¼ teaspoon ground ginger
¼ teaspoon salt
1 cup flaked coconut
½ cup chopped pecans or walnuts (optional)
sugar glaze (optional)

Sugar Glaze

1 cup powdered sugar, sifted
1 teaspoon vanilla
5 to 6 teaspoons milk

Preheat oven to 350°F. In a large bowl, cream butter, sugars, and vanilla until light and creamy. Add eggs and milk; beat well. Stir in beans. In another bowl, mix flours, baking soda, baking powder, cinnamon, nutmeg, cloves, ginger, and salt. Stir dry ingredients into wet ingredients. Add coconut and nuts if using. Pour into a greased Bundt pan. Bake for 50 to 55 minutes.

For glaze, combine ingredients, add milk to desired consistency. Drizzle over cooled cake.

Variation

Bake the pinto spice cake in a greased 9 x 13-inch baking dish for 30 minutes or until toothpick inserted in center comes out clean.

Pinto Bean Pecan Pie

Serve this pie with ice cream or whipped cream.

½ cup butter, room temperature
2 eggs
1 cup sugar
½ cup brown sugar
1 cup cooked pinto beans (may use 1 cup of canned pinto beans), well mashed or pureed
¼ cup maple syrup or corn syrup
1 teaspoon vanilla
1 cup chopped pecans
1 unbaked 9-inch pie shell

Preheat oven to 375°F. In a large bowl, mix butter, eggs, and sugars until creamy. Add mashed pinto beans, syrup, vanilla, and pecans. Pour into unbaked pie shell. Bake for 25 minutes. Reduce heat to 350°F and bake 20 minutes more.

Variation

Pinto Bean Chocolate Pecan Pie: Sprinkle 1 cup semisweet chocolate chips over unbaked pie crust. Pour pinto bean mixture over chocolate chips and bake as directed above. Yum!

Strawberry Crunch Parfait

Sweet, creamy, and crunchy.

2 cups (1 pint) plain yogurt
⅓ to ½ cup maple syrup
2 cups rolled oats
1 cup sliced almonds
½ cup sunflower seeds
½ cup maple syrup
¼ teaspoon salt
½ teaspoon cinnamon
¼ cup vegetable oil
4 cups frozen strawberries, slightly thawed, quartered
1 cup sugar

Line a strainer with paper towels or cheesecloth and place over a bowl so strainer doesn't touch bottom. Pour yogurt into strainer, cover with plastic wrap, and let drain, refrigerated, 4 hours or overnight.

In a bowl, place thickened yogurt and add maple syrup to taste.

Set aside in refrigerator.

Preheat oven to 325°F. In a large bowl, combine oats, sliced almonds, sunflower seeds, maple syrup, salt, cinnamon, and oil. Spread evenly in a jelly roll pan with sides. Bake for about 30 minutes, stirring occasionally. Cool to room temperature.

Place strawberries and sugar in a large saucepan. Bring to a boil over medium heat. Cook, stirring, until strawberries and sugar become juicy. Reduce heat and simmer, uncovered, 6 to 8 minutes or until slightly thickened. Cool to room temperature.

To assemble; spoon 3 tablespoons strawberry mixture into parfait glasses or dessert dishes. Top with 2 tablespoons granola, 2 tablespoons yogurt. Repeat layering.

Store remaining granola in an airtight container.

Quick Tip: Use any family favorite granola.

Peach Ice Milk

Light and refreshing.

1 cup powdered milk
½ cup sugar
1 ½ cups water
1 teaspoon vanilla
5 to 6 ripe peaches: peeled, pitted, and cut
   into chunks

In a food processor or blender, puree ingredients until smooth.

Pour milk mixture into ice-cream maker. Freeze according to manufacturer's directions.

Serve ice milk softly frozen, or package airtight and freeze up to 2 days. Let stand at room temperature 10 to 15 minutes to soften before scooping.

Pumpkin Chocolate Cookies

Moist and spicy, these cookies have a lot of flavor.

1 cup sugar
½ cup brown sugar
1 cup butter, room temperature
1 egg, lightly beaten
1 teaspoon vanilla
1 cup quick oats
1 cup whole-wheat flour
1 cup all-purpose flour
1 teaspoon baking soda
1 teaspoon cinnamon
½ teaspoon ground ginger
¼ teaspoon ground cloves
1 cup pumpkin
1 cup semisweet chocolate chips

Preheat oven to 350°F. In a large bowl, beat sugars and butter until creamy (2 to 3 minutes). Add egg and vanilla, beat well. Combine the oats, flours, baking soda, cinnamon, ginger, and cloves. Mix dry ingredients into the creamed mixture alternately with pumpkin. Fold in chocolate chips. Drop by tablespoons onto a greased or parchment-lined cookie sheet. Bake for 10 to 12 minutes. Let cool 5 minutes before removing to wire rack.

Snickerdoodles

A classic my family never tires of.

½ cup butter or margarine, room temperature
½ cup shortening
1½ cups sugar
2 eggs, room temperature
2¾ cups flour
1 teaspoon baking soda
2 teaspoons cream of tartar
½ teaspoon salt
2 teaspoons cinnamon
3 tablespoons sugar

Preheat oven to 400°F. In a bowl, with an electric mixer on medium, beat butter, shortening, and sugar until light and fluffy. Add eggs and combine. Stir in flour, baking soda, cream of tartar, and salt until thoroughly combined.

Shape by rounded teaspoonfuls into balls.

Mix cinnamon and sugar in a small bowl; roll balls in mixture. Place about 2 inches apart on ungreased or parchment lined cookie sheet.

Bake for 8 to 10 minutes. Cool 1 minute; remove from cookie sheet to a wire rack.

Note: A true classic Snickerdoodle uses half butter and half shortening. Look for shortenings that do not contain partially hydrogenated oil.

Pinto Bean Fudge

Melt in your mouth delicious and nobody guesses the secret ingredient.

1 can (15 oz.) pinto beans, drained well
¼ cup milk
1 tablespoon vanilla
6 tablespoons butter
6 oz. unsweetened chocolate
2 lbs. powdered sugar, sifted

Place pinto beans in food processor and puree well with milk to the consistency of mashed potatoes. Transfer to large bowl and add vanilla. Melt butter and chocolate in double boiler (bring water to a boil and then turn to low heat), stirring occasionally. Stir chocolate mixture into bean mixture. Gradually stir in powdered sugar, kneading with hands if necessary to blend thoroughly. Spread into a lightly greased 9-inch baking dish. Chill for 2 hours. Cut into squares and serve. Store in refrigerator.

Never "scoop" flour. Always spoon the flour into your measuring cup, sprinkling it lightly, then level with a knife. Scooping flour will pack flour into the measuring cup, and as a result you usually end up with too much flour in your recipe.

Texas Sheet Cake

2 cups sugar

2 cups flour

1 cup butter

4 tablespoons cocoa powder

1 cup water

½ cup buttermilk (or ½ cup milk with ½ tablespoon vinegar)

2 eggs, slightly beaten

1 teaspoon baking soda

1 teaspoon cinnamon

1 teaspoon vanilla

Preheat oven to 400°F. Put sugar and flour in mixing bowl. Melt together butter, cocoa, and water until butter is melted. Add to sugar and flour and blend. Whip together buttermilk and eggs and add to other ingredients. Add soda, cinnamon, and vanilla. Bake in a jelly roll pan for 14 minutes. Do not grease pans. Frost with Cocoa Icing while hot.

Cocoa Icing

¼ cup butter

4 tablespoons cocoa

5 tablespoons milk

1 lb. box powdered sugar (about 3 ¾ cups)

1 teaspoon vanilla

1 cup broken pecans (optional)

In saucepan combine butter, cocoa, and milk. Bring to boil and simmer while cake is baking. Remove from heat and stir in remaining ingredients. Blend well and spread on hot cake. Best if blended with a hand mixer until smooth.

Toffee Nut Bars

Rich and irresistible.

1 cup butter or margarine, room temperature

1 cup brown sugar

1 ½ teaspoons vanilla

1 cup whole-wheat flour

1 cup all-purpose flour

1 cup semisweet chocolate chips

1 cup chopped pecans or walnuts

Preheat oven to 350°F. In a large bowl, combine butter and brown sugar with an electric mixer until light and creamy. Add vanilla and flours; mix well. Stir in chocolate chips and pecans. Press mixture into an ungreased jelly roll pan with sides. Bake for 25 minutes or until lightly browned. Score bars with knife while slightly warm. Remove bars when cool.

Scotch Oat Bars

These bars whip up so quickly and easily, they have become a favorite after-school snack.

1 cup butter or margarine
4 cups quick oats
1 cup brown sugar
½ cup white sugar
2 teaspoons baking powder
1 teaspoon vanilla
½ teaspoon salt

Preheat oven to 350°F. In a large saucepan, melt butter over low heat. Remove from heat. Add oats, sugars, baking powder, vanilla, and salt. Mix well. Pat into a greased 9 x 13-inch baking dish. Bake 25 to 28 minutes or until golden brown. Cool and cut into bars.

Variation

Drizzle cooled bars with melted semisweet chocolate. Cool. Cut into bars.

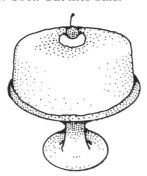

Zucchini Chocolate Cake

½ cup butter, room temperature
½ cup buttermilk
¼ cup oil
1¾ cup sugar
2 eggs
1 teaspoon vanilla
2½ cups flour (try 1½ cups wheat and 1 cup white)
4 tablespoons cocoa powder
1 teaspoon baking soda
½ teaspoon cinnamon
½ teaspoon salt
2 cups zucchini, peeled and shredded
1 to 2 cups chocolate chips

Preheat oven to 325°F. Mix together butter, buttermilk, oil, and sugar until smooth. Add eggs and vanilla and blend together. Mix in the dry ingredients and, last, fold in zucchini.

Pour in ungreased jelly roll pan and top with chocolate chips. Bake for 25 minutes. Let cool and dust with powdered sugar.

Sugar Cookies

Soft and delicious.

 1 ½ cups powdered sugar
 1 cup butter, room temperature
 1 egg
 1 teaspoon vanilla
 1 teaspoon almond extract
 2 ½ cups flour
 1 teaspoon baking soda
 1 teaspoon cream of tartar

Preheat oven to 375°F. Beat powdered sugar, butter, egg, vanilla and almond extract in a medium mixing bowl until smooth and creamy. In a separate bowl, mix flour, baking soda and cream of tartar. Mix dry ingredients into creamed mixture. Wrap dough in plastic wrap and refrigerate 3 hours. Roll dough out to ¼ inch thick on lightly floured surface. Cut into desired shapes with cookie cutters. Place on lightly greased or parchment lined baking sheet and bake for 7 to 8 minutes. Frost with Creamy Vanilla Frosting.

Creamy Vanilla Frosting

 3 cups powdered sugar
 ⅓ cup butter
 1 ½ teaspoons vanilla
 2 tablespoons milk

Beat powdered sugar and butter. Add vanilla and milk and beat until smooth and spreadable consistency. May add food coloring.

Fun Ideas: Roll dough into balls and press a large baking chip (they come in a variety of colors at the craft stores) in the middle. Color the dough and coordinate colors for the holidays (i.e. red or green dough with red or green baking chips, or use pastel colors for springtime, etc.)

Variation

Chocolate Sugar Cookies: Add 2 tablespoons of baking cocoa. Top chocolate cookie with large white or chocolate baking chip or mint flavored baking chip.

Vanilla Ambrosia Ice Cream

Rich, creamy, and irresistible.

 4 eggs, beaten well
 1 ½ cups sugar
 1 can (14 oz.) sweetened condensed milk
 2 cans (12 oz. each) evaporated milk
 2 tablespoons vanilla
 1 teaspoon salt
 1 cup powdered milk

In a 2 quart pitcher (8 cups), mix eggs, sugar, sweetened condensed milk, evaporated milk, vanilla, salt, and powdered milk until well combined. Add enough water to make 2 quarts total and mix well. Pour into ice cream maker and process according to directions. May need to freeze for several hours before serving. Serves 8 to 10.

Variations

After processed in ice cream maker but before serving or before freezing, mix in one or none of these additions.

- ½ cup strawberry jam or family favorite jam
- ½ cup mini chocolate chips (with or without ¼ cup peanut butter)
- ¾ to 1 cup chopped candy bar
- ¾ to 1 cup crushed Oreo cookies

Family Meals

When parting advice to young newlyweds I often encourage them to learn to cook and learn to love it. Food is a part of our lives everyday and will be everyday for the rest of our lives. Meals bring families together. They facilitate closeness within families creating a time to communicate and connect.

In fact, I believe family dinner is as essential to sustaining a healthy family lifestyle as food is to sustaining life! Oftentimes, mealtime is the reason our children come home. Regular family dinner brings a sense of security and stability to each family member. As a mother, I am greatly satisfied and rewarded as our family sits down together at the end of each day, eating a healthy and delicious meal while sharing our individual experiences.

When no family dinner is prepared, just the opposite happens. Family members mill around in the kitchen often choosing less healthy alternatives while interacting with no one. They are not satisfied physically or emotionally. Regular dinners not only provide the occasion for families to be together but also the opportunity to use and rotate our stored foods. And yes, it can be absolutely delicious.

Vanilla Pudding

Great over fresh or canned fruit.

½ cup sugar
2 tablespoons cornstarch
6 tablespoons powdered milk
⅛ teaspoon salt
1¼ cups water
1 teaspoon vanilla
2 tablespoons butter

Whisk sugar, cornstarch, powdered milk, and salt in heavy saucepan. Add water and stir over medium heat until thick stirring constantly. Cook and stir for 1 to 2 minutes.

Remove from heat. Add vanilla and butter. Serve warm or pour into bowl and press with plastic wrap and refrigerate. Makes 4 servings.

Variation

Add a dash of nutmeg or cinnamon.

Hot pudding will typically form a "skin" on top as it cools. You can prevent it by placing a piece of plastic wrap or waxed paper directly on the surface of the hot pudding. After it cools, remove the wrap.

Chocolate Peanut Butter Cream Parfaits

A sublime combination of flavors.

1 recipe cooled Chocolate Pudding (p. 75)
1½ cups heavy cream, divided
3 tablespoons powdered sugar
½ teaspoon vanilla
¼ cup smooth peanut butter
4 Peanut Butter Cookies (p. 83)
⅓ cup chopped peanuts (optional)

Whip 1 cup heavy cream, powdered sugar, and vanilla in a medium bowl with electric mixer until soft peaks form. Set aside.

In another bowl, stir peanut butter and remaining ½ cup heavy cream (unwhipped), until smooth. Fold in whipped heavy cream until combined.

Into 4 tall glasses, create alternating layers by spooning cooled chocolate pudding using spring-loaded ice cream scoop or ¼ cup measuring cup and whipped cream mixture. Cover and chill 2 hours or overnight. Crumble peanut butter cookies over each parfait, sprinkle with chopped peanuts if desired. Serves 4.

Drinks & Smoothies

Frosty Vanilla Drink

A perfect treat.

1 ½ cups very cold water
1 ½ cups instant powdered milk
½ cup sugar
1 tablespoon vanilla
20 ice cubes

Place all ingredients in the blender and blend on high for 2 full minutes. Serve immediately. Makes four 12 oz. servings.

Variations

French Vanilla: Crack an egg into the shake before blending.

Fruit: Add any fruit (fresh or canned). Try strawberry-banana, fresh mango, crushed pineapple, or very berry (blueberry, strawberry, raspberry). Frozen berries will make the drink thicker.

Ice Cream Vanilla Shake: Add a scoop of vanilla ice cream.

Any-Jar-of-Fruit Smoothie

Vary the sweetness of this smoothie by the choice of fruit sweetened in syrup or fruit juice.

2 cups bottled fruit, with juice, chilled
1 frozen banana, broken into chunks
1 cup yogurt
4 ice cubes

In a blender combine fruit, banana, and yogurt. Blend until creamy. Add ice cubes and blend. Serve immediately. Serves 2.

Berry-Peach Smoothie

This smoothie is light and delicious, kids love it.

1 ½ cups milk
1 cup frozen blueberries or raspberries
1 cup frozen sliced peaches
1 banana
½ cup plain yogurt
1 tablespoon pure maple syrup

In a blender, combine milk, blueberries, peaches, banana, yogurt, and maple syrup. Cover and process until well blended. Serves 2.

Grape Shake

Completely refreshing.

- 1 apple, peeled and cored
- 1 banana
- 1 cup seedless grapes, red or green
- 2 cups orange juice
- 10 ice cubes

Add all ingredients to blender and whirl on high until smooth. Serve immediately.

Tip: Freeze the grapes and use less ice.

Creamy Grape Shake: Add ½ cup vanilla yogurt.

Chocolate Milk

Tastes like store bought.

- 8 cups water
- 2¼ cups instant powdered milk
- ¼ cup cocoa powder, sifted
- ½ cup sugar
- pinch salt
- ½ teaspoon vanilla

Mix ingredients together. Chill overnight and serve cold. Makes ½ gallon.

Frosty Chocolate Drink

A rich chocolate drink without the guilt.

- 1 ½ cups very cold water
- 1 ½ cups instant powdered milk
- ½ cup sugar
- ¼ cup Dutch cocoa powder
- 1 teaspoon vanilla
- 20 ice cubes

Place all ingredients in the blender and blend on high for 2 full minutes. Serve immediately. Makes four 12 oz. servings.

Variations

Chocolate Banana: Add one banana.

Chocolate Peanut Butter: Add ¼ cup (large spoonful) of peanut butter.

Chocolate Mint: Add ¼ teaspoon peppermint extract.

Ice Cream Chocolate Shake: Go ahead, add a scoop of vanilla ice cream.

To add punch of protein to any smoothie, add 2 tablespoons of protein powder.

Breakfast Smoothie

A great way to start any day.

    1 fresh banana
    6 to 8 frozen strawberries
    3 cups vanilla soy milk
    ½ cup orange juice concentrate
    1 to 2 tablespoons ground flaxseed
    3 to 4 ice cubes

Blend and serve.

This smoothie is packed with vitamin C, calcium, fiber, and those important omega 3 fatty acids, and it's delicious to boot!

Note: You can purchase soy milk that is shelf stable at most grocery or warehouse stores. It is easy to store and has a shelf life of a year or longer. I love that it does not have to be refrigerated until it is opened. What a great way to add to your milk food storage!

Hot Chocolate Mix

The cinnamon and vanilla add just the right touch.

    10 cups instant powdered milk
    3 cups powdered sugar, sifted
    1 cup granulated sugar
    2½ cups Dutch cocoa powder, sifted
    2 tablespoons cinnamon
    2 tablespoons powdered vanilla

Mix together and store in airtight container. To use, mix ¼ cup of hot chocolate mix for every 1 cup of water or milk, then heat to desired temperature. Powdered milk mixes best when mixed with a whisk rather than a spoon. Stir with a cinnamon stick or a peppermint stick. If desired, top each mug with a dollop of whipped cream and a dusting of cocoa.

Note: Most hot chocolate mixes contain a creamer. However, creamers contain partially hydrogenated fat, as do most commercial hot chocolate mixes. This homemade hot chocolate mix has a smooth creamy feel although it has no creamer.

Tip: You can find powdered vanilla in most natural food stores.

Our Cocoa Taste Test

There is a difference in the taste and flavor of cocoa powder. In our taste test, a rich, Dutch-processed cocoa fared much better than the more common Hershey's cocoa. The most noticeable difference was in the non-baked items such as hot chocolate, chocolate smoothies, frostings, etc.

Orange Julius

Pleasantly refreshing.

2 cups water
8 tablespoons instant powdered milk
¼ cup sugar
4 oz. frozen orange juice concentrate
1 teaspoon vanilla
12 ice cubes

Whirl in blender. Serve.

I first discovered this recipe using 1 cup cream and 1 cup milk. Absolutely fabulous! However, in my quest to cut out fat I started using 2 cups milk, which made a lighter version and was still delicious. Then I started substituting powdered milk and water for the fluid milk. Excellent alternative! If it is too "powdered milk tasting" for your family, use one cup fluid milk with 1 cup water and 4 tablespoons powdered milk.

Pineapple Spinach Smoothie

Green and surprisingly delicious.

2 cups fresh spinach leaves, packed
2 cups pineapple juice
1 banana
15 ice cubes

Whirl all ingredients in blender until well combined (about one full minute). This drink turns out to be bright green but tastes like pineapple banana. A great way to get your greens! This is a fun drink to serve on St. Patrick's Day.

> You can vary the sweetness of your smoothie by the ripeness of the banana or other fruit.

Spiced Drink Mix

A drink to share with any friend.

1 cup orange drink mix (Tang)
½ cup powdered lemonade
1½ teaspoons cinnamon
¾ teaspoon ground cloves
1½ cups sugar

Combine all ingredients and store in an air tight container.

To use: Combine 1 heaping spoonful of Spiced Drink Mix with one cup boiling water. Stir until mix has dissolved completely.

Strawberry-Mango Smoothie

This is a great morning starter or after-school snack.

2 cups frozen strawberries
1 cup frozen chopped mango
1 banana
1 ½ cups plain or vanilla yogurt
1 ½ cups milk

In a blender, combine the strawberries, mango, banana, yogurt, and milk. Cover and process until well blended. Serves 2.

Strawberry Breakfast Shake

Try using soy, rice, or almond milk in this special shake.

2 cups orange juice (can use from concentrate)
½ cup milk
½ cup vanilla yogurt
1 package (10 oz.) slightly thawed frozen strawberries
4 ice cubes

In a blender, combine the orange juice, milk, yogurt, and strawberries. Cover and process until well blended. Add the ice cubes; cover and process until smoothie reaches desired consistency. Serves 2.

Main Dishes

Italian Meatballs

A perfect complement to pasta.

   1 ½ lbs. ground turkey or beef
   2 eggs, lightly beaten
   ¼ cup evaporated milk
   ¾ cup dried bread crumbs
   ⅓ cup Parmesan cheese, grated
   2 tablespoons dried parsley
   ½ teaspoon garlic powder
   ¼ teaspoon onion powder
   ½ teaspoon basil
   ¼ teaspoon thyme
   ½ teaspoon salt
   ¼ teaspoon pepper

Preheat oven to 425°F. In a large bowl, combine all ingredients thoroughly. Roll into 1 ½-inch meatballs (about 24). Place on a greased jelly roll pan with sides. Bake for 20 minutes until browned.

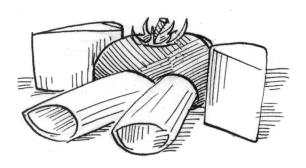

Baked Penne Pasta

Scrumptious!

   1 lb. penne pasta
   1 cup vegetable oil
   9 garlic cloves, minced fine
   1 large onion, chopped
   ½ teaspoon red pepper flakes
   1 tablespoon oregano
   3 tablespoons basil
   1 teaspoon marjoram
   2 teaspoons sugar
   3 cans (28 oz. each) whole or diced tomatoes
   ¾ cup Parmesan cheese, grated

In a large bowl, place pasta and pour oil over, stirring well. Allow pasta to sit uncovered at room temperature for 1 hour, stirring occasionally. In a strainer over a large saucepan, drain pasta. Set pasta aside. Add garlic, onion, red pepper flakes, oregano, basil, marjoram and sugar to oil. Over medium heat, cook mixture 10 minutes or until oil is very hot. Remove from heat and cool. In a food processor or by hand, crush tomatoes. Add tomatoes and pasta to oil mixture; mix well. Pour into an 11 x 17-inch baking pan. Bake at 400°F for 40 minutes, stirring every 10 minutes, to ensure pasta cooks evenly. To serve, sprinkle with Parmesan cheese. Serves 6 to 8.

Baked Chimichangas

2 lbs. beef stew meat, boneless chicken, or
  pork loin
1 ½ cups water
¼ teaspoon garlic powder
2 tablespoons chili powder
1 tablespoon vinegar
2 teaspoons dried oregano
1 teaspoon salt
⅛ teaspoon pepper
1 teaspoon ground cumin
8 to 10 flour tortillas (10 inch)

Toppings (optional)

Monterey Jack or cheddar cheese, grated
Guacamole
Sour cream
Salsa
Shredded lettuce

Preheat oven to 350°F. In a medium saucepan
combine meat, water, garlic, chili powder, vinegar,
oregano, salt, pepper, and cumin. Bring to a boil.
Cover and reduce heat to a simmer and cook for
2 hours or until meat is tender. Uncover and boil
rapidly about 15 minutes, stirring occasionally.

Using two forks, shred meat. Spoon about ⅓ cup
of meat onto each warm tortilla near one edge.
Fold tortilla over filling just until meat is covered. Fold in both sides, envelope style, and roll
up. Place seam side down in 9 x 13-inch baking
pan. Bake uncovered for 15 to 20 minutes until
tortillas are crisp and lightly browned. Top with
desired toppings.

Delightful Apricot Chicken
A delicious combination of flavors.

6 boneless, skinless chicken breasts
1 bottle (8 oz.) Thousand Island salad dressing
1 packet dry onion soup mix
1 small jar apricot jam

Preheat oven to 350°F. Place chicken in one layer in a greased 9 x 13-inch baking pan. Spoon a
heaping spoonful of salad dressing on top of each
chicken breast. Stir onion soup mix and sprinkle
on top of salad dressing. Then, spoon one large
spoonful of jam on top of each. The layers blend
together nicely during baking for a delicious and
delightful flavor. Bake for 1 hour. Serves 6.

Variation

The more common version of this dish is to
use Russian dressing, dry onion soup mix, and
apricot jam that have been whisked together and
poured over chicken. Both are great.

Beans in a Pot

A substantial and satisfying meal. Try adding salsa, cheese, and sour cream.

1 lb. dry white, pinto, or pink beans, sorted
  and rinsed
6 cups water
1 medium onion, finely chopped
2 cloves garlic, minced
1 serrano or jalapeno pepper, seeded and
  finely chopped
2 tablespoons vegetable oil
1 ½ teaspoons salt

In a deep pot, place beans and water; simmer 2 minutes. Cover and let stand 1 hour. Don't drain. Add onion, garlic, chopped pepper, oil, and salt. Bring mixture to a boil; simmer for 1 ½ to 2 hours or until beans are soft. Add more boiling water if needed.

Variation

Refried Beans: Heat 3 to 5 tablespoons of oil over medium-heat in a large skillet (preferably nonstick); add ½ medium onion, chopped, and cook stirring until tender, about 4 minutes. Stir in 2 cloves garlic, minced, and 1 teaspoon chili powder and cook for 1 minute. Add ½ to ¾ cup broth and ½ lb. cooked beans and cook until beans are warmed. Mash beans with a potato masher and add more broth to desired consistency. Add salt and pepper to taste.

Corn Tortillas

2 cups corn masa mix or corn flour
1 to 1 ½ cups water

Mix the corn masa with water in medium bowl until soft and like play dough. Roll a piece of dough into a golf-ball sized ball. Using a tortilla press or two pieces of plastic wrap, press evenly until about ⅛ inch thick, it may be necessary to rotate tortilla 180 degrees and press a second time. If the tortilla appears to be crumbling, add a little water to dough. Place tortilla on a hot pancake griddle. Bake for 1 to 1 ½ minutes on each side.

Makes about 12 tortillas.

Popcorn can be ground in your wheat grinder (check manufacturer's directions) to make corn flour.

Beef Zucchini Skillet Dinner

Great served with crusty bread and salad.

2 tablespoons oil
1 lb. ground beef
1 medium onion, chopped
1 garlic clove, minced
2 medium zucchini, halved and sliced
1 can (14.5 oz.) diced tomatoes
1 can (15 oz.) whole kernel corn, drained
½ cup mild salsa
1 teaspoon basil
¼ teaspoon oregano
Salt and pepper to taste
½ cup Parmesan cheese, grated

In a large skillet, heat oil. Add ground beef, onion, and garlic over medium heat and cook until beef is no longer pink. Drain any excess fat. Stir in zucchini, diced tomatoes, corn, salsa, basil, oregano, and salt and pepper. Bring to a boil over medium heat. Reduce heat to a simmer and cover. Cook for 15 minutes or until zucchini is tender. Simmer uncovered 5 to 10 minutes to reduce liquid if needed. Sprinkle with Parmesan cheese. Serves 6.

Variation

Turkey Zucchini Skillet Dinner: Replace ground beef with ground turkey.

Chicken and Rice Burritos

Another winning skillet dish and a great way to use left-over brown rice.

½ green pepper, diced
½ red pepper, diced
1 tablespoon olive oil
1 can (15 oz.) corn, drained
1 can (15.5 oz.) black beans, drained
3 cups cubed cooked chicken
1 ½ cups cooked brown rice, cooked in 1 teaspoon chicken bouillon
¾ cup chunky salsa
½ lime, freshly squeezed
grated cheese (cheddar or mozzarella)
tortillas

Sauté peppers in olive oil until soft. Add corn, beans, chicken, brown rice, and salsa and mix to heat through. Spritz with fresh lime juice. Melt ¼ cup cheese on tortilla in microwave. Spoon rice mixture on tortilla and roll burrito style. Serve warm.

The best way to cook and cube chicken for recipes: Place thawed chicken breasts on baking tray. Sprinkle with salt and pepper. Bake at 350°F for 28 minutes. Let sit for 10 minutes. Cut into cubes.

Chicken Enchiladas

Enchilada Sauce

 1 can (15 oz.) tomato sauce
 dash salt and pepper
 1 tablespoon sugar
 2 ½ tablespoons flour
 2 ½ tablespoons chili powder
 3 tablespoons butter

Enchiladas

 2 cups chicken, cooked and chopped
 1 cup sour cream
 2 oz. diced green chilies (canned)
 1 cup chopped onions
 2 tablespoons butter
 ½ teaspoon Mrs. Dash seasoning
 3 cups shredded cheddar cheese
 8 flour tortillas
 sliced olives for garnish (optional)
 chopped green onion for garnish (optional)

Put all enchilada sauce ingredients in a medium saucepan and bring to a boil. Remove from heat.

Preheat oven to 350°F. Combine chicken, sour cream, and green chilies. Set aside. In another pan, sauté onions in butter until golden. Add onion, Mrs. Dash, and 2 cups cheese to chicken mixture. Spoon 2 tablespoons of enchilada sauce on each tortilla and spread to edges. Top the sauce on each with ⅓ cup of chicken mixture. Roll up and place close together in a lightly sprayed 9 x 13-inch pan. Cover with remaining enchilada sauce and shredded cheese. Bake uncovered for 20 to 25 minutes. Garnish with sliced olives and chopped green onions. Serve hot. Makes 8.

If tortillas are too long to fit in baking pan, trim edges on either side of tortilla before filling and rolling.

Chicken Supreme
Familiar flavors make this dish a family favorite.

 4 to 6 chicken breasts, skinless and boneless
 4 to 6 slices Swiss cheese
 1 can (10.75 oz.) cream of chicken soup
 ½ cup water
 2 cups seasoned stuffing
 ⅓ cup butter, melted

Preheat oven to 325°F. Place chicken in a 9 x 13-inch baking pan. Top each piece with a slice of cheese.

Thin soup with water and pour over chicken. Mix stuffing with melted butter and sprinkle over chicken. Bake for 1 hour 15 minutes.

Chicken Veggie Rice Bowl

You can substitute brown rice in this flavorful rice bowl. Increase chicken broth to 2¼ cups.

1 cup uncooked white rice
1¾ cup chicken broth
2 tablespoons vegetable oil
1 medium onion, thinly sliced
1 small green pepper, cut into ½-inch strips
¾ cup corn
½ cup peas
2 cups cooked chicken breast, chopped
1 teaspoon basil
¼ teaspoon oregano
½ teaspoon rubbed sage
salt and pepper to taste

In a large saucepan, combine rice and chicken broth. Bring to a boil, reduce heat to low, and simmer for 15 to 20 minutes or until water is absorbed and rice is tender. (Simmer 45 minutes if using brown rice.)

Place oil in a large skillet over medium heat, sauté onion and green pepper 5 to 6 minutes, stirring occasionally. Add corn, peas, chicken, basil, oregano, sage, and salt and pepper.

Simmer for 5 minutes or until heated through. Stir in rice and chicken and serve. Serves 4.

Creamy Parmesan Pasta

1 can (10.5 oz.) cream of chicken soup
1 can (10.5 oz.) milk (fill empty soup can)
4 oz. cream cheese
1 teaspoon garlic powder
1 teaspoon basil
1 cup Parmesan cheese, grated
½ lb. pasta, cooked and drained

Combine soup, milk, cream cheese, garlic powder, and basil in saucepan over medium heat. Bring sauce to a simmer, stirring occasionally. Cook until cream cheese is melted. Remove from heat. Stir in Parmesan cheese and stir until melted and combined. Pour over cooked pasta.

Variation

Sun-Dried Tomato Chicken Pasta: After creamy Parmesan cheese is melted, add 2 boneless, skinless chicken breast (cooked and chopped), ¼ to ⅓ cup julienned sun-dried tomatoes, and 1 cup chopped zucchini (steamed, sauteed, or grilled).

Serve over angel hair pasta.

Parmesan Garlic Chicken

Make extra to have a tasty sandwich later.

1 packet (1 oz.) zesty Italian salad dressing mix
½ cup Parmesan cheese, grated
¼ teaspoon garlic powder
4 boneless skinless chicken breasts

Preheat oven to 400°F. In a shallow bowl, combine salad dressing mix, Parmesan cheese, and garlic powder. Moisten chicken with water. Dip chicken in the cheese mixture, turning to coat pieces thoroughly.

Place chicken on a greased jelly roll pan. Bake, uncovered, for 20 to 25 minutes or until chicken is tender. Serves 4.

Crustless Zucchini Pie

A great dish to use the zucchini you don't know what to do with.

¼ cup butter
1 tablespoon oil
4 cups zucchini, thinly sliced
1 medium onion, chopped
2 teaspoons dried parsley
½ teaspoon salt
¼ teaspoon pepper
½ teaspoon Italian seasoning
½ teaspoon garlic powder
3 large eggs, beaten
2 cups mozzarella cheese, grated
¼ cup Parmesan cheese, grated

Preheat oven to 375°F. In a large skillet, melt butter with oil. Add zucchini and onion. Cook and stir over medium heat for 8 to 10 minutes or until onion and zucchini are soft. Add parsley, salt, pepper, Italian seasoning, and garlic powder. In small bowl, combine eggs and mozzarella cheese. Stir egg mixture into zucchini mixture. Pour into a greased 10-inch glass pie plate. Sprinkle Parmesan cheese evenly over top. Bake for 20 minutes or until set. Serves 4 to 6.

Easy Shepherd's Pie

Another hit with the kids.

 1 lb. ground beef or turkey
 1 medium onion, chopped
 1 tablespoon flour
 1 cup water
 1 teaspoon beef bouillon
 1 cup frozen peas
 1 cup carrots, chopped
 1 tablespoon Worcestershire sauce
 1 teaspoon salt
 ½ teaspoon pepper
 4 cups instant mashed potatoes, prepared according to package directions
 1 cup grated cheddar or jack cheese

Preheat oven to 375°F. In a skillet, brown ground beef or turkey and onion. Drain fat. Sprinkle cooked meat with flour and stir. Add water and beef bouillon and mix; bring to a boil. Reduce heat to low, add peas, carrots, Worcestershire sauce, salt and pepper. Mix together.

Simmer uncovered 5 minutes. Spray a 9 x 13-inch baking pan with cooking spray. Pour meat mixture into pan. Spread mashed potatoes evenly over top. Sprinkle with cheese.

Bake for 25 to 30 minutes until bubbling and brown.

Hawaiian Chicken

A fantastic chicken recipe.

 1 can (8 oz.) crushed pineapple
 ½ cup ketchup
 ½ cup butter
 ¼ cup white vinegar
 ¼ cup brown sugar
 1 tablespoon soy sauce
 2 tablespoons cornstarch
 ½ teaspoon salt
 ¼ teaspoon pepper
 5 boneless, skinless chicken breast halves
   (about 6 oz. each)
 ¼ cup shredded coconut
 ½ cup slivered almonds, toasted

Preheat oven to 350°F. In a saucepan, combine pineapple, ketchup, butter, vinegar, brown sugar, soy sauce, cornstarch, salt, and pepper. Heat over medium heat, stirring until butter is melted and sauce is smooth and thickened.

Place chicken breasts in a greased 9 x 13-inch pan. Bake for 30 minutes. Pour pineapple sauce over chicken. Sprinkle with coconut and almonds. Bake 20 minutes longer. Serve with rice. Serves 6.

Haystacks

Guests build their own haystacks by placing a mound of rice on plate, spooning on chicken sauce, and adding toppings as desired.

Sauce

   2 tablespoons butter
   ½ cup chopped onion
   2 cans (10.75 oz. each) cream of chicken soup
   6 cups cooked and diced chicken
   2 cups sour cream
   8 cups cooked rice

Toppings

   mandarin oranges
   pineapple tidbits
   slivered almonds
   water chestnuts
   chopped celery
   chopped green onion
   pine nuts
   chopped peppers (green/red/yellow)
   peas
   tomatoes
   mushrooms
   coconut
   chow mein noodles

For sauce, sauté butter and onions in saucepan for about 3 minutes. Add chicken soup and warm over medium heat. Stir in chicken and sour cream and cook until hot, but do not boil.

Pork Chop and Rice Casserole

   4 to 6 pork chops
   oil
   1 can (10.75 oz.) cream of chicken soup
   1 packet dry onion soup mix
   1 cup water
   1 cup uncooked white rice

Preheat oven to 325°F. In a skillet, brown pork chops in oil, about 2 minutes per side. In a medium bowl, mix cream of chicken soup, onion soup mix, and water together until well blended. Add rice and stir. Spray 9 x 13-inch baking dish with non-stick spray. Pour rice mixture into dish. Place chops on top. Cover with foil. Bake for 1 hour and 15 minutes. Serves 4 to 6.

Variation

Use 4 to 6 boneless, skinless chicken breasts in place of pork chops.

Honey Mustard Chicken

A great flavor combination.

  1 cup dried plain bread crumbs
  3 tablespoons honey
  ¼ cup Dijon mustard
  1 tablespoon lemon juice
  4 boneless, skinless chicken breast halves
    (about 6 oz. each)
  1 to 2 tablespoons vegetable oil

Preheat oven to 375°F. Place bread crumbs in a shallow dish. Mix honey, mustard, and lemon juice in a shallow dish. Dip chicken into mustard mixture and coat both sides. Dredge in bread crumbs, pressing to coat chicken.

Place in a jelly roll pan sprayed with cooking spray. Drizzle oil evenly over each chicken breast. Bake for 20 to 25 minutes, or until cooked through. Serves 4.

Lasagna Roll Ups

A twist on classic lasagna.

  1 package (10 oz.) frozen chopped spinach,
    thawed and squeezed dry
  1 cup (4 oz.) shredded part-skim mozzarella
    cheese
  1 carton (15 oz.) whole-milk ricotta cheese
  ¾ cup Parmesan cheese, grated and divided
  1 egg, lightly beaten
  ¼ teaspoon salt
  ¼ teaspoon freshly ground pepper
  12 lasagna noodles, cooked and drained
  1 jar (26 oz.) pasta sauce

Preheat oven to 350°F. In a bowl, combine the spinach, mozzarella, ricotta cheese, ½ cup Parmesan, egg, salt, and pepper. Spread a ⅓ cupful evenly over each noodle. Roll up and secure with toothpicks.

Place seam side down in a 9 x 13-inch baking dish coated with non-stick spray. Pour pasta sauce over roll-ups. Cover and bake for 35 minutes or until bubbly. Sprinkle with remaining Parmesan cheese. Discard toothpicks.

Oven Meatballs

Makes 72 meatballs. Freeze in quantities of 24 and use with one of the delicious sauces below for three quick and easy meals or appetizers.

3 beaten eggs
¾ cup milk
3 cups soft bread crumbs (try using whole-wheat bread crumbs)
½ cup finely chopped onion
2 teaspoons salt
3 lbs. ground beef or turkey

Preheat oven to 375°F. In a large mixing bowl combine beaten eggs, milk, bread crumbs, chopped onion, and salt. Add ground beef and mix well. Shape into 1-inch balls (about 6 dozen). Bake for 25 to 30 minutes. You will need to bake 36 at a time on a jelly roll pan. Remove from pan and let cool. Freeze on cookie sheet until firm and then bag 24 meatballs in freezer bag, seal, and label. You will have three bags of 24 meatballs.

Appetizer Meatballs

1 cup concord grape jelly
1 cup chili sauce
⅓ recipe Oven Meatballs (p. 110)

In a large saucepan, combine grape jelly and chili sauce over medium low heat. Add meatballs and simmer, covered, for 20 minutes, stirring occasionally. Serve on platter with a toothpick inserted in each meatball.

Stroganoff Meatballs

1 can (10.75 oz.) cream of chicken soup
¾ cup milk
1 package (3 oz.) cream cheese, softened
2 tablespoons ketchup
⅛ teaspoon garlic powder
⅛ teaspoon ground thyme
⅓ recipe frozen Oven Meatballs (p. 110)
1 cup sour cream
8 oz. medium egg noodles, cooked and drained

Combine soup and milk in large saucepan. Add cream cheese, ketchup, garlic powder, and thyme. Stir over low heat until blended. Stir in frozen meatballs and simmer, covered, for 20 minutes, stirring occasionally. Stir in sour cream and heat through without boiling. Serve over cooked noodles. Sprinkle with paprika. Serves 4 to 6. This recipe is nice over rice, too.

Quick Thaw for Chicken: Soak frozen chicken breasts in cool water for 30 minutes. Pat dry. Use kitchen shears to remove any extra skin or fat. Bake as called for in recipe.

Sweet and Sour Meatballs

1 can (13.75 oz.) pineapple tidbits

½ cup brown sugar

3 tablespoons cornstarch

1 cup water

⅓ cup vinegar

1 beef bouillon cube

1 tablespoon soy sauce

1 green pepper, cut into chunks

1 can (5 oz.) sliced water chestnuts, drained

1 carrot, sliced on the diagonal

⅓ recipe frozen Oven Meatballs (p. 110)

cooked rice (see Perfect Brown Rice, p. 142)

Drain pineapple, reserving syrup. In a large saucepan mix brown sugar and cornstarch. Blend in reserved pineapple syrup, water, vinegar, bouillon, and soy sauce. Cook and stir until thick and bubbly. Stir in frozen meatballs, pineapple, green pepper, water chestnuts, and carrot. Sim-

mer covered, 20 minutes, until meatballs are heated through and vegetables are tender, stirring occasionally. Serve over rice. Serves 4 to 6.

Oven "Fried" Chicken

Watch this chicken disappear.

1 cup biscuit/baking mix

1 packet onion soup mix

¼ teaspoon pepper

4 boneless, skinless, chicken breast halves (about equal size) or 6 boneless, skinless chicken thighs

3 tablespoons butter, melted

Preheat oven to 350°F. Combine biscuit mix, onion soup mix, and pepper in a shallow bowl. Dampen chicken slightly with water. Dip chicken breast into biscuit mixture, pressing biscuit mixture to chicken, and shake off excess. Place chicken on a greased jelly roll pan with sides. Drizzle each chicken breast evenly with melted butter. Bake for 50 to 55 minutes or until chicken is tender.

Tip: When selecting chicken, buy pieces of equal size so they will cook evenly at the same time. If some pieces are large and some small, the small ones will dry out by the time the larger pieces are fully cooked.

Sprouting

If you haven't heard about the nutritional content of sprouts, you are in for a surprise. Sprouts are perhaps the most living and complete food on earth loaded with live enzymes, vitamins, minerals, chlorophyll, protein and fiber.

As seeds absorb water and begin to sprout, an amazing chemical change occurs. A tremendous energy is released and the natural complex carbohydrates and proteins stored in the seed are turned into enzymes, essential amino acids, vitamins, and minerals. Vitamin A, vitamin C, vitamin E and vitamin B complex which are almost non-existent in the seed, explode as the seed sprouts increasing significantly, nearly sixfold in some cases. Minerals and trace elements become easily digestable and chlorophyll, created by the sun's energy within the sprout, becomes a powerhouse for cells in the human body when consumed. And the best part? You can grow this arsenal of nutrition in your own home in less than a week.

Sprouting is easy and not only great for everyday living but essential in an emergency situation. Sprouts give us the fresh nutrition needed when no other garden or produce is available. Sprouting seeds store for long periods of time and should be part of everyone's food storage plan.

Commercial sprouters are inexpensive and easy to use, however, you can sprout seeds in jars, trays, and sprouting bags. Almost any whole seed, nut, or bean can be sprouted. Try sprouting alfalfa, lentils, mung beans, chick peas, whole-wheat berries, raw almonds, raw sesame seeds, raw sunflower seeds, millet, adzuki beans, cabbage, red clove, radish, buckwheat, arugula, fenugreek seed. Don't wait for an emergency to start sprouting. Master this skill now and add sprouts to salads, sandwiches, wraps, stir fry, or eat them raw. Delicious and perhaps the healthiest food on the planet!

My favorite commercial sprouter is the Kitchen Crop. It has three sprouting trays allowing for three varieties of sprouts. Also, each tray of sprouts can be started at different times so you always have a fresh crop of sprouts ready to eat.

Lasagna

1 lb. ground turkey or beef
½ lb. Italian sausage
1 clove garlic, minced
1 tablespoon dried basil
1¼ teaspoons salt
1 can diced tomatoes
2 cans (6 oz. each) tomato paste
1 cup water
12 oz. lasagna noodles (14 noodles)
2 eggs
3 cups ricotta cheese
½ cup Parmesan cheese, grated
2 tablespoons parsley flakes
1 teaspoon salt
½ teaspoon pepper
1 lb. (4 cups) mozzarella cheese, grated

Brown meats slowly and spoon off excess fat. Add garlic, basil, salt, tomatoes, tomato paste and water. Simmer, covered, 15 minutes stirring often. Cook noodles in boiling water until tender; drain. In medium bowl, beat eggs with fork and add remaining ingredients, except mozzarella.

Preheat oven to 375°F. Layer half the noodles in a 9 x 13-inch baking dish; spread with half the ricotta filling; sprinkle with half the mozzarella and then half the meat sauce. Repeat. Bake for 40 minutes. May assemble early and refrigerate; bake 45 to 60 minutes. Let stand 10 minutes before serving.

Pizza-Smothered Chicken and Vegetables

A busy-night skillet dish that is sure to hit the spot.

1 can (14.5 oz.) chicken broth
4 oz. dried vermicelli or other thin pasta, broken into thirds
10 oz. mixed vegetables (stir-fry vegetables work well)
4 boneless, skinless chicken breasts
½ teaspoon dried basil
1 cup pizza sauce (or pasta sauce)
⅛ to ¼ teaspoon crushed red pepper flakes
½ cup mozzarella cheese, grated
2 tablespoons Parmesan cheese, grated

In large skillet, bring the broth to a boil over high heat. Stir in the pasta and vegetables. Top with chicken and sprinkle with basil. Spoon pizza sauce over chicken and sprinkle with red pepper flakes. Return to a boil. Reduce heat and simmer covered for 10 minutes or until chicken is no longer pink in the center. Cook uncovered until liquid is absorbed (5 to 10 minutes). Sprinkle mozzarella over the chicken and sprinkle Parmesan over all. Serve hot. Makes 4 servings.

Lime Tortilla Chicken

The best of Mexican flavors.

1 cup finely crushed plain tortilla chips (for best results, crush in food processor or blender)
2 tablespoons vegetable oil
2 tablespoons lime juice
1 teaspoon honey
6 boneless, skinless, chicken breasts (about 6 oz. each)
1 can (14.5 oz.) mexican stewed tomatoes
1 teaspoon dried cilantro (or 2 tablespoons fresh)
¼ teaspoon chili powder
¼ teaspoon garlic powder
1 cup Jack cheese, shredded

Preheat oven to 350°F. Place finely crushed tortilla chips on plate. Combine oil, lime juice, and honey in a shallow bowl. Dip chicken breasts in oil mixture, then press in chips. Place in a greased jelly roll pan with sides. Bake for 25 minutes or until chicken is cooked through.

While chicken bakes, puree tomatoes, cilantro, chili powder and garlic powder together in food processor or blender to make a sauce.

Remove chicken from oven and spread evenly with sauce. Sprinkle with cheese. Continue baking until cheese melts, about 5 to 8 minutes. Serves 6.

Classic Sloppy Joes

A definite crowd pleaser.

2 lbs. ground beef
1 medium onion, chopped
1 green pepper, chopped
1 teaspoon salt
½ teaspoon pepper
½ teaspoon dry mustard
½ teaspoon chili powder
1 clove garlic, minced (or ⅛ teaspoon garlic powder)
1 cup ketchup
4 tablespoons brown sugar
1 tablespoon Worcestershire sauce
2 tablespoons apple cider vinegar
½ teaspoon Tabasco sauce

In large frying pan, brown meat, onion and green pepper, stirring occasionally. Drain fat, and add remaining ingredients. Simmer covered 20 to 30 minutes, stirring occasionally. Serve on toasted buns.

Lemon Chicken

Lightly-breaded, seasoned chicken and a tangy lemon sauce make an absolutely mouthwatering combination.

1 cup flour
1 teaspoon seasoned salt
6 boneless, skinless chicken breast halves
   (about 6 oz. each)
3 tablespoons vegetable oil
½ cup lemon juice
1 teaspoon lemon zest (outer yellow part only,
   finely grated)
½ cup sugar
1 ½ tablespoons cornstarch
¼ teaspoon salt
1 cup water

Preheat oven to 350°F. Combine flour and seasoned salt in a plastic zip top bag. Add chicken and shake until chicken is completely coated with flour mixture. Heat oil in large skillet over medium-high heat. Brown chicken on both sides, about 3 to 4 minutes a side. Set aside.

In a bowl, whisk lemon juice, lemon zest, sugar, cornstarch, and salt. Slowly add water until thoroughly mixed and no lumps remain. Place chicken in a greased 9 x 13-inch baking pan. Pour lemon sauce over chicken and bake for 20 to 25 minutes. Serves 6.

Tamale Pie Casserole

Slightly spicy and so delicious.

¾ cup cornmeal
1 large egg, beaten
1 ½ cups milk
2 tablespoons vegetable oil
1 lb. ground turkey or beef
1 medium onion, chopped
1 can (10 oz.) mild enchilada sauce
½ teaspoon oregano
1 can (14.5 oz.) diced tomatoes, undrained
1 can (15 oz.) whole kernel corn, undrained
1 ½ cups Jack or cheddar cheese, shredded

Preheat oven to 350°F. In a large bowl, combine cornmeal, egg, and milk. Set aside. Heat oil in a large skillet, brown ground turkey until no longer pink. Drain excess fat. Add onion, enchilada sauce, oregano, diced tomatoes, and corn. Simmer over medium heat for 5 minutes. Stir meat mixture into cornmeal mixture. Pour into a greased 2 ½ quart casserole dish. Bake for 45 to 50 minutes. Sprinkle with grated cheese, bake until cheese is melted. Serves 6.

Stuffed Jumbo Shells

A hearty meal to satisfy everyone's hunger.

1 package (12 oz.) jumbo shells
2 lbs. ground beef or turkey
1 medium onion, finely chopped
4 eggs
1 cup seasoned bread crumbs (1 cup bread crumbs with ½ teaspoon seasoned salt)
1 cup mozzarella cheese, shredded
½ cup Parmesan cheese, grated and divided
¾ teaspoon dried oregano leaves
½ teaspoon salt
¼ teaspoon pepper
¼ teaspoon garlic powder
1 jar (about 25 to 28 oz.) pasta sauce

Preheat oven to 375°F. Cook pasta according to directions on package. In a large skillet, brown meat and onion over medium heat until meat is thoroughly cooked and onions are soft; drain fat.

In a large bowl, stir together cooked meat mixture, eggs, seasoned bread crumbs, mozzarella cheese, ¼ cup Parmesan cheese, oregano, salt, pepper, and garlic powder. Spread ½ cup of pasta sauce on the bottom of a 9 x 13-inch pan.

Stuff cooked shells with about 1½ tablespoons of meat filling each and layer on top of sauce (you may need to layer the shells on top of each other). Spread remaining sauce over shells and sprinkle with the remaining Parmesan cheese. Cover with foil and bake for 40 minutes.

Spaghetti Sauce

Serve with pasta and Italian Meatballs (p. 100), a green salad, and Parmesan Breadsticks (p. 44).

2 tablespoons vegetable oil
1 small onion, finely chopped
3 garlic cloves, minced
1 can (15 oz.) tomato sauce
1 can (6 oz.) tomato paste
1 can (28 oz.) crushed tomatoes
1 cup beef broth (can also use chicken broth)
½ teaspoon Worcestershire sauce
1 tablespoon sugar
1 teaspoon dried parsley
1 teaspoon basil
½ teaspoon oregano
1 teaspoon salt
¼ teaspoon pepper

In a large saucepan, combine all the sauce ingredients and bring to a boil over medium heat. Reduce heat to low, cover, and simmer 1 hour, stirring occasionally. Serve over pasta.

Chicken Teriyaki Rice Bowl

Use this recipe as a variation on the Chicken Veggie Rice Bowl on page 105.

Prepare rice, replacing chicken broth with 1¾ cup water and ½ teaspoon salt.

Omit corn, peas, basil, oregano, sage, salt and pepper.

Add:

1 medium carrot, peeled, cut into strips (2 x ½-inch) to skillet with onion and green pepper. Cook stirring occasionally for 7 to 9 minutes or until vegetables are tender. Add 1 bag (12 oz.) frozen broccoli flowerets, cook 5 to 6 minutes stirring frequently until broccoli is tender. Add chicken to skillet and cook until heated through. Stir in ½ to ⅔ cup teriyaki glaze (see recipe below) or use your favorite stir- fry sauce. Let cook about 1 minute. Serve over cooked rice or cooked ramen noodles. Sprinkle with 1 tablespoon sesame seeds if desired.

Teriyaki Glaze

⅔ cup soy sauce
1 cup pineapple juice
¼ cup ketchup
½ cup sugar
3 tablespoons rice vinegar
2 tablespoons honey
Pinch red pepper flakes
2 garlic cloves, crushed in a garlic press
¼ teaspoon ground ginger

In a large saucepan, combine soy sauce, pineapple juice, ketchup, sugar, rice vinegar, honey, red pepper flakes, garlic and ginger.

Bring to a boil over medium heat. Reduce heat to low, simmer and cook, stirring, until thickened, about 18 to 20 minutes.

Makes about 1 cup.

Store poultry immediately after purchase in the refrigerator, for no longer than two days or wrap in foil, label, and freeze up to 6 months.

Twice-Dipped Chicken Parmesan

3 large eggs
¼ teaspoon salt
¼ teaspoon pepper
3 cups dried bread crumbs, plain or seasoned
6 boneless, skinless chicken breast halves
¼ cup olive oil
3 cups pasta sauce, divided
½ cup Parmesan cheese, grated
shredded mozzarella cheese
1 tablespoon dried parsley

Preheat oven to 350°F. In a shallow bowl, whisk together eggs with salt and pepper. Put breadcrumbs on a sheet of wax paper. Dip the chicken in the egg mixture and then in crumb mixture to coat. Dip the coated chicken in the egg mixture again and then coat with bread crumbs again.

Heat oil in a large nonstick skillet over medium-high heat. Add chicken and cook for 4 minutes, turning once, until golden brown. Meanwhile, place 2 cups of the pasta sauce in a 9 x 13-inch baking pan. Place browned chicken in sauce-lined pan, cover with remaining 1 cup pasta sauce. Sprinkle with cheeses and parsley. Bake for about 15 to 20 minutes or until chicken is cooked through. Serves 6.

Turkey Patties

Savory, yet delicate, these Turkey Patties make a delicious skillet dish.

1 lb. ground turkey (or beef)
⅓ cup dry bread crumbs
½ teaspoon salt
¼ teaspoon pepper
1 egg
1 onion, diced
1 can (10.5 oz.) consommé soup
1 can (4 oz.) mushrooms, drained
2 tablespoons cold water
1 tablespoon cornstarch

Mix ground turkey, bread crumbs, salt, pepper, and egg. Shape into 4 or 5 oval patties, each about ¾ inch thick. Cook patties in skillet over medium heat, turning occasionally, until brown on both sides, about 10 minutes. Drain. Add onion, soup, and mushrooms. Heat to boiling. Reduce heat and cover. Simmer until beef is done, about 10 minutes.

Remove patties and keep warm. Heat onion mixture to boiling. Mix water and cornstarch in separate bowl and stir into onion mixture. Boil and stir 1 minute until thickened. Serve over patties.

Flaxseed

"Adding flaxseeds to your diet may help to ward off heart disease. In a recent study, men and women with high cholesterol ate muffins with either flaxseeds or a wheat bran placebo for three weeks each. Participants who ate flaxseeds showed decreases in LDL cholesterol, compared to little change in the placebo group." ("Fight Back with Food," *Reader's Digest, p.73)*

Add one tablespoon of ground flaxseeds to your pancake or waffle batter or to your cookie or muffin dough. You can stir ground flaxseed into your hot oatmeal or add to meatballs and meatloaves. Add a tablespoon to your smoothies. However you do it, flaxseed will add a much needed punch of nutrition to your diet.

Flaxseeds are rich in alpha-linolenic acid (ALA), which is the major omega-3 fatty acid. Because our bodies cannot manufacture ALA and must be consumed through foods in our diet, it is known as an essential fatty acid. Flaxseeds also contain soluble and insoluble fiber and lignans, all of which play vital roles in optimal health.

Flaxseed can be found in the health section of most grocery stores. You can purchase it in either the golden or dark variety. The nutrition content is the same, however, golden flaxseed is typically more expensive. It is best to grind the flaxseed in a coffee or nut and seed grinder for maximum nutrition. Our bodies do not process the whole flaxseed, thus we do not reap the full benefit unless it is ground. Keep whole flaxseed in the refrigerator and grind only what you intend to immediately use. Larger quantities of flaxseed can be stored in the freezer.

Asian Chicken

This chicken bakes in a tangy sauce for an easy oven dish.

4 boneless, skinless chicken breast halves
   (about 6 oz.)
Salt and pepper
2 large eggs, beaten
1 cup flour

Sauce

¾ cup ketchup
2 tablespoons soy sauce
⅔ cup sugar
¼ cup cider vinegar
½ teaspoon salt
½ teaspoon ground ginger
½ teaspoon garlic powder

Preheat oven to 400°F. Sprinkle chicken with salt and pepper. Place eggs and flour in two separate shallow dishes. Dip chicken breasts in beaten egg; dredge in flour. Place chicken on a greased jelly roll pan with sides.

Mix sauce ingredients until blended. Pour over each chicken breast. Bake for 25 to 30 minutes or until chicken is cooked through. Serves 4.

Yogurt Parmesan Chicken

Moist and delicious.

6 to 8 chicken breasts, boneless, skinless
2 cups finely ground bread crumbs
2 tablespoons Parmesan cheese, grated
1 teaspoon seasoned salt
1 teaspoon garlic powder
2 cups plain yogurt
2 tablespoons butter, melted

Preheat oven to 350°F. Trim fat from chicken and pat dry. Mix bread crumbs, Parmesan cheese, seasoned salt, and garlic powder in small bowl. Dip each chicken breast in the yogurt then coat with the seasoned bread crumb mixture. Place in a 9 x 13-inch pan and drizzle melted butter over chicken. Bake for 40 to 45 minutes until chicken is cooked through. Serve with Creamy Honey Mustard Dipping Sauce (page 121) on the side.

Using whole-wheat bread crumbs is not only a way to add whole grains to your diet but also helps to use up old bread. Grind bread in advance and freeze.

Creamy Honey Mustard Dipping Sauce

½ cup sour cream
2 tablespoons Dijon mustard
1 tablespoon honey
salt and pepper to taste

Combine all ingredients. Serve with Yogurt Parmesan Chicken.

Baked BBQ Chicken with Bacon

Sure to please everyone.

1 large yellow onion, thinly sliced and separated into rings
6 boneless, skinless chicken breasts (about 6 oz. each)
1 cup Sweet Honey BBQ Sauce (see recipe below) or favorite barbecue sauce
6 bacon slices, chopped into 2-inch pieces

Preheat oven to 350°F. In a greased 9 x 13-inch baking pan, spread onions evenly. Lay chicken breasts atop the onion rings. Brush barbecue sauce over each chicken breast and top each piece with chopped bacon. Bake for 1 hour, basting with sauce twice while chicken is baking.

Sweet Honey BBQ Sauce

1 onion, finely chopped
2 tablespoons butter
1 can (8 oz.) tomato sauce
¼ cup brown sugar
¼ cup honey
2 tablespoons Worcestershire sauce
2 tablespoons molasses
1 teaspoon dry mustard
¼ teaspoon salt
½ teaspoon chili powder
1 tablespoon cider vinegar
1 tablespoon water

Sauté onion in butter until soft. Add remaining ingredients and stir to thoroughly combine. Let simmer over low heat for 15 minutes, stirring occasionally.

Mexican Meatballs

A tasty twist to the traditional meatball.

1 lb. ground turkey or beef
½ cup finely crushed tortilla chips
½ cup grated zucchini, optional
¼ cup green onions, finely chopped
1 large egg, lightly beaten
½ teaspoon ground cumin
½ teaspoon garlic powder
½ teaspoon oregano
Salt and pepper to taste
1 can (10 oz.) mild enchilada sauce
½ cup water

Preheat oven to 375°F. In a large bowl, mix all ingredients except enchilada sauce and water. Shape into 1½-inch meatballs. Place on a sprayed baking sheet with a rim. Bake for 20 minutes or until browned.

In a large skillet, combine enchilada sauce and water. Add cooked meatballs, bring to a boil, reduce heat to low, cover and simmer for 5 minutes. Serve over rice. Serves 4.

Lamb Chops with Orange Barbecue Glaze

Fast to fix and fabulous.

½ cup barbecue sauce
⅓ cup orange juice concentrate
¼ teaspoon ground ginger
4 lamb chops, about 1 inch thick

Mix barbecue sauce, orange juice concentrate, and ginger in a small saucepan. Bring to a simmer over medium heat, cook for 2 to 3 minutes, stirring occasionally. Set aside ⅓ cup for serving as a sauce with the cooked lamb chops. Place lamb chops on a broiler pan, brush remaining sauce over both sides of lamb chops.

Broil 10 to 12 minutes on each side or until meat reaches desired doneness. Serve warm with reserved sauce.

Tip: When selecting lamb chops, buy shoulder or loin chops, instead of the thicker, smaller French chops. Look for shoulder lamb chops that are about 1 inch thick. They will cook evenly when broiled.

Sweet and Spicy Glazed Pork Chops

Tangy and terrific.

6 pork chops, 1 inch thick
2 tablespoons cornstarch
¼ cup apple juice
¼ cup soy sauce
½ teaspoon ground ginger
⅓ cup ketchup
½ cup brown sugar
1 ¼ cup apple juice

Preheat oven to 350°F. Place pork chops in a greased baking pan that just fits 1 layer of the pork chops.

Bake for 45 minutes. Pour off fat and juices. Keep oven on.

In a saucepan, stir together cornstarch and ¼ cup apple juice until smooth. Over medium heat, add soy sauce, ginger, ketchup, brown sugar, and 1 ¼ cup apple juice. Simmer, stirring constantly until lightly thickened. Immediately pour over pork chops. Bake in hot oven for 10 to 15 minutes. Serves 6.

Turkey Meatloaf

Where's the beef? Leave it behind with this delicious and healthy alternative.

¾ cup green onion, chopped
¾ cup yellow onion, chopped
½ cup bell pepper, chopped
2 garlic cloves, minced
2 eggs
½ cup ketchup
½ cup milk
1 tablespoon + 1 teaspoon Worcestershire sauce
½ teaspoon salt
2 lbs. ground turkey
12 oz. turkey sausage
½ cup bread crumbs
¼ cup ketchup

Preheat oven to 375°F. Sauté onions, pepper, and garlic in frying pan. Set aside. In large bowl, mix together eggs, ketchup, milk, Worcesterchire sauce, salt, turkey, and bread crumbs.

Add onion mixture to meat mixture just until blended. Line a 9 x 13-inch pan with foil. Shape meatloaf into a loaf 12 inches long by 5 inches wide and 2 inches high. Brush with ketchup. Bake for 1 hour 15 minutes. Internal temperature of meatloaf should be 155°F.

Teriyaki Pan Salmon

Unbelievably fast and easy, with just the right amount of spice.

- 4 salmon skinless filets (approximately 6 oz. each), completely thawed
- 2 tablespoons oil
- 2 tablespoons brown sugar
- 2 teaspoons ground ginger
- 2 teaspoons garlic powder
- 1 teaspoon cayenne pepper
- 1 ½ tablespoons teriyaki sauce

In a large frying pan, heat oil over medium-high heat, tilting pan to coat. In a small bowl combine brown sugar, ginger, garlic powder, and cayenne pepper. Add teriyaki sauce and stir to mix thoroughly. Brush mixture on both sides of salmon and place in hot oil. Reduce heat to medium. Cook salmon on each side for 3 minutes. Serve immediately. Makes 4 servings.

Easy Baked Pork Chops with Chunky Apple Compote

This sweet and salty combo is dynamite!

Pork Chops

- 6 pork chops, ½ inch thick
- 1 package dry onion soup mix

Chunky Apple Compote

- 3 apples, peeled, cored and chopped
- ½ cup apple cider or apple juice
- 2 tablespoons brown sugar
- ¼ teaspoon cinnamon
- pinch of cloves
- pinch of nutmeg
- pinch of salt

Preheat oven to 350°F. Pour dry soup mix into a shallow bowl. Pat both sides of each pork chop with dry soup mix and place in a 9 x 13-inch baking dish. Bake until no longer pink in center, about 20 to 30 minutes. Do not overbake. Remove from oven, turn each chop over and let sit 2 minutes.

For Chunky Apple Compote, place all ingredients in a medium saucepan over medium-high heat. Bring to a boil. Reduce heat and simmer 15 to 20 minutes until apples are tender and liquid is absorbed. Serve over hot pork chops.

Salads

Barbecue Chicken Salad

A hearty salad full of flavor and texture. Great for a festive luncheon or dinner.

8 oz. mixed baby greens
1 small head romaine, chopped
2 cups cooked chicken breast, chopped
1 can (15 oz.) black beans, drained and rinsed
1 can (15 oz.) corn, drained or 2 cups frozen corn, thawed
1 small red onion, finely chopped
1 medium tomato, chopped
1 ½ cups mozzarella cheese, shredded
1 ripe avocado, chopped
Salt and pepper to taste
1 to 2 cups tortilla chips, broken
Dressing choices: Use half ranch salad dressing and half barbeque sauce combined to taste *or* combine 4 tablespoons vegetable oil, 3 tablespoons vinegar or lime juice, and ⅓ cup barbeque sauce until mixed well.

In a large serving bowl, toss baby greens, romaine, chopped chicken breast, black beans, corn, red onion, tomato, mozzarella cheese, and avocado. Drizzle dressing of choice on salad. Toss gently. Add salt and pepper to taste and chips if desired, toss again gently. Serves 4 to 5.

Best Bean Salad

Colorful and healthy.

2 cans (16 oz. each) cut green beans
1 can (16 oz.) garbanzo beans
1 can (16 oz.) kidney beans
1 can (16 oz.) wax beans
1 can (16 oz.) whole kernel corn
½ cup sugar
½ teaspoon salt
¼ teaspoon dry mustard
¼ cup olive oil
¾ cup apple cider vinegar
1 medium red onion, diced

Drain beans and corn thoroughly and combine in a large bowl. In separate bowl, mix sugar, salt, dry mustard, oil, vinegar, and diced onion. Pour mixture over vegetables. Stir together, and chill two hours or overnight before serving. Serves 12.

Wax beans can be found in any grocery store. Wax beans are yellow in color and look like a cut green bean.

Bow Tie Pasta Salad

This great make-ahead salad is sure to please everyone.

1 lb. bow tie pasta
Italian dressing (try Bernstein's Restaurant
  Italian Recipe dressing)
2 cups chopped cooked chicken breast
1 can (15 oz.) garbanzo beans, drained
1 can (15 oz.) black olives, drained and halved
½ cup drained, chopped sun-dried tomatoes
  (packed in oil)
6 green onions, chopped
¼ cup celery, thinly sliced
1 cup (4 oz.) feta cheese, crumbled
¾ cup Parmesan cheese, grated

Bring a large pot of salted water to a boil over high heat. Add the pasta and cook according to the package directions.

Drain the pasta thoroughly in a colander, then transfer it to a large bowl. Add a little of the salad dressing, toss, and let pasta cool. Add the rest of the ingredients and toss gently before serving. Serves 6 to 8.

> When boiling pasta, add 2 tablespoons of salt to the water after the water has come to a boil.

Chicken Pasta Caesar Salad

An absolute crowd pleaser.

3 cups chopped cooked chicken breast
3 cups romaine lettuce, sliced
½ lb. penne pasta, cooked
1 cup grape tomatoes
4 green onions, finely chopped
¼ cup chopped fresh parsley or 1 tablespoon
  dried parsley
1 cup (4 oz.) feta cheese, crumbled
1 minced garlic clove
½ cup Caesar dressing

In a serving bowl, combine salad ingredients. Toss with Caesar dressing to coat. Serves 4.

Chicken Strawberry Salad

A beautiful showcase that tastes as good as it looks.

Chicken

6 boneless, skinless, chicken breasts
1 cup Italian dressing
1 cup Lawry's Mesquite-Lime Marinade
1 cup teriyaki sauce
lemon pepper to taste

Strawberry Vinaigrette

1 teaspoon salt
1 teaspoon pepper
8 tablespoons sugar
8 tablespoons vinegar
1 cup oil
8 tablespoons strawberry jam

Sweet and Spicy Pecans

¼ cup sugar
1 cup warm water
1 cup pecans
2 tablespoons sugar
1 tablespoon chili powder
⅛ teaspoon ground red pepper

Salad

mixed greens
green onions
sweetened strawberries
diced apples (tossed with fresh lime juice)
spiced pecans
crumbled feta cheese

Combine Italian salad dressing, Mesquite Marinade, and teriyaki sauce in a gallon-sized, zipper-sealed bag. Add chicken breast and marinate in refrigerator for at least 2 hours. Transfer chicken to a jelly roll pan and sprinkle with lemon pepper. Bake at 350°F for 28 minutes or until done. Let rest on pan for 10 minutes. Thinly slice. Discard remaining marinade.

In a small bowl, mix vinaigrette ingredients together. Set aside.

For pecans, stir sugar and water together until sugar dissolves. Soak pecans in mixture for 10 minutes.

Mix together sugar, chili powder, and red pepper. Drain pecans from first mixture and coat in second mixture. Place pecans on greased cookie sheet and bake at 350°F for 10 minutes.

On a large platter, toss together mixed greens, green onions, and a little of the dressing. Place thinly sliced chicken down the center.

Around periphery, place sliced sweetened strawberries, diced apples, spiced pecans, and crumbled feta cheese. Drizzle with vinaigrette just before serving.

Mixed Baby Greens with Pears
Simple and impressive.

Dressing

    ½ cup vegetable oil
    ¼ cup vinegar
    ¼ cup sugar
    ½ teaspoon dry mustard
    ¼ cup cranberries
    salt and pepper to taste

Candied Walnuts

    ½ cup coarsely chopped walnuts
    2½ tablespoons sugar

Salad

    8 cups (5 oz.) mixed baby greens
    1 cup (4 oz.) feta cheese, crumbled
    ¼ cup dried cranberries
    1 (29 oz.) can pears halves, drained, and sliced
    or 2 to 3 fresh pears, peeled and thinly sliced

For dressing, combine oil, vinegar, sugar, dry mustard, cranberries, and salt and pepper in blender. Whirl until smooth and completely blended.

In a small skillet, place walnuts and sugar over medium heat and stir with wooden spoon constantly until sugar melts and walnuts are lightly brown. Watch carefully.

Place mixed greens, feta cheese, and cranberries in large salad bowl.

To serve, toss salad with dressing to taste, and top with sliced pears and candied walnuts. Serves 6 to 8.

Pineapple Green Salad

A terrific combination of ingredients.

Salad

>   1 head romaine lettuce, washed and chopped
>   2 avocados, halved, peeled, cut in chunks
>   1 fresh pineapple, peeled, cut into chunks

Poppy Seed Dressing

>   ½ cup sugar or pure maple syrup
>   1 teaspoon dry mustard
>   1 medium onion, minced
>   ¼ cup vinegar
>   ¾ teaspoon salt
>   1 to 2 tablespoons poppy seeds
>   1 cup vegetable oil

Candied Almonds

>   ½ cup sliced almonds
>   2½ tablespoons sugar

In a large bowl, combine lettuce, avocados, and pineapple. In another bowl, combine all dressing ingredients except oil. Slowly add oil until well blended. To make candied almonds, place almonds and sugar in a medium skillet over medium heat and stir constantly with wooden spoon until sugar melts and almonds are lightly browned. Toss lettuce mixture with poppy seed dressing. Add candied almonds and toss gently, serve immediately. Serves 4 to 6.

Try with canned, drained pineapple chunks if fresh isn't available.

Light Ranch Salad Dressing

>   1 cup mayonnaise
>   1 cup plain yogurt
>   ¼ cup milk
>   1 tablespoon dry onion
>   1 teaspoon dried parsley
>   1 teaspoon pepper
>   ½ teaspoon salt
>   ¼ teaspoon garlic powder

Whisk all ingredients together until smooth. Cover. Refrigerate and let set for 30 minutes. Store in refrigerator.

Taco Salad

A complete meal that's great for lunch or dinner.

Salad

 2 tablespoons oil
 1 lb. ground turkey or beef
 3 tablespoons taco seasoning mix
 ¼ cup water
 1 head romaine lettuce, washed and sliced
 1 can (16 oz.) black beans, rinsed and drained
 1 can (15 oz.) whole-kernel corn, drained
 1 pint cherry tomatoes (about 25)
 1 cup grated cheddar or jack cheese
 1 avocado, halved, peeled, cut in chunks
 2 cups tortilla chips

Dressing

 ½ cup Italian dressing
 ½ cup Ranch dressing

Heat oil in a nonstick skillet, add meat and brown. Drain off any fat. Add taco seasoning mix and water. Cook over medium heat, stirring frequently, until water is absorbed.

In a large bowl add meat mixture and the rest of the ingredients except chips and dressing. Combine dressing ingredients and add to the salad. Toss gently to mix and coat. Sprinkle each serving with chips. Serves 4.

Try combining romaine with mixed baby greens for variety.

Visiting Teaching Chicken Salad

A definite hit with the ladies.

 3 cups cooked diced chicken *or* 2 cans
  (12.5 oz. each) canned chicken
 1 cup purple grapes, halved
 ½ cup diced celery
 ⅓ cup slivered almonds or cashews
 ¼ cup diced green onions

Sauce

 ⅓ cup apricot jam
 ⅓ cup real mayonnaise
 ⅛ teaspoon curry powder

In a large bowl, combine chicken, grapes, celery, almonds, and green onion. For sauce, thoroughly blend ingredients. Toss sauce to taste over chicken salad and gently mix to coat just before serving. Serve on croissants. Enjoy!

Time Saving Tip: Use pre-cooked chicken strips and cut into pieces.

Ramen Salad

A salad with a crunch.

Salad

    1 package chicken Top Ramen noodles
    ½ head iceberg lettuce, chopped
    ½ head green cabbage, chopped
    ¼ cup sliced almonds, toasted
    2 tablespoons sunflower seeds, toasted
    4 green onions, chopped

Dressing

    Seasoning packet from noodles
    2 tablespoons sugar
    ½ cup oil
    3 tablespoons vinegar
    1 teaspoon salt
    ½ teaspoon pepper

Place Ramen noodles in a plastic bag and coarsely crush with rolling pin or meat mallet. Combine lettuce, cabbage, Ramen noodles, almonds, sunflower seeds, and green onions in large salad bowl. Mix dressing together and shake well to combine. Toss salad with desired amount of dressing and serve immediately.

Tasty Tip: Try a combination of vinegars (i.e. rice, white, and/or balsamic).

Transport Tip: Mix dressing beforehand and refrigerate. Chop lettuce, cabbage and green onions and store in large plastic bag. Mix almonds and sunflowers seeds in small bag. Transport to destination and toss together in salad bowl just before serving.

Rice and Black Bean Salad

You can make this salad up to one day ahead of time; chill covered.

    1½ cups cooked white basmati rice, cooled
    1 can (15 oz.) black beans, rinsed and drained
    1 cup carrots, diced
    1 red bell pepper, chopped
    1 can (8 oz.) whole kernel corn, drained
    ½ red onion, diced
    1 tablespoon dried parsley

Dressing

    3 tablespoons red wine vinegar
    ¼ cup vegetable oil
    1 teaspoon Dijon mustard
    salt and pepper to taste

In serving bowl, combine rice, black beans, carrots, red pepper, corn, red onion, and parsley.

For dressing, stir vinegar, oil, Dijon mustard, and salt and pepper. Toss rice mixture with dressing just before serving. Serves 4 or 5.

Garlic Croutons

Excellent way to use up old bread.

5 cups cubed bread (6 to 8 slices of bread)
¼ cup butter, melted
¼ cup olive oil
2 teaspoons fresh minced garlic (or ½ teaspoon garlic powder)
¼ teaspoon onion powder
¼ teaspoon garlic powder
¼ teaspoon paprika
pinch of salt
¼ teaspoon Italian Seasoning (optional)

Preheat oven to 350°F. Cut crusts off bread and cut into cubes. Set aside. In large bowl, melt butter. Add olive oil, garlic, and seasonings. Mix thoroughly. Add bread cubes and gently toss to coat evenly. Bake on baking sheet for 20 minutes or until golden and lightly crispy, turning once with spatula during baking. Let cool and dry on pan. Store in airtight container and refrigerate unused portions. Use as a salad or soup topper.

Pineapple Gelatin Salad

This sweet and tangy jello-like salad has no added sugar.

6 envelopes Knox gelatin
1 can (46 oz.) unsweetened pineapple juice
1 can (14 oz.) unsweetened crushed pineapple
½ cup juice sweetened pineapple jam
whipped cream (optional)
fresh raspberries (optional)

In a bowl, sprinkle gelatin over 2 cups pineapple juice. Let stand one minute to soften. In a saucepan, boil 3 cups of pineapple juice and juice with softened gelatin, until gelatin is dissolved. Add the rest of the juice, crushed pineapple, and jam. Pour into 9 x 13-inch pan. Refrigerate at least 4 hours or overnight. Cut into 9 squares. Top with fresh raspberries and whipped cream, if desired.

Asian Chicken Salad

This combination of great flavors makes this salad a favorite.

2 cups spinach leaves, stemmed

3 cups romaine and/or iceberg lettuce, chopped

3 green onions, chopped

1 can (11 oz.) mandarin oranges, drained

2 tablespoons pine nuts

2 tablespoons sliced almonds, toasted

2 tablespoons sunflower seeds, toasted

2 cups chicken, chopped (or use rotisserie chicken)

Sesame Dressing, see recipe below or use bottled dressing, Feast from the East

Sesame Dressing

⅓ cup rice vinegar

⅓ cup vegetable oil

1 tablespoon sesame oil

2 tablespoons sugar

1 tablespoon soy sauce

½ teaspoon ground ginger

1 teaspoon dry mustard

¼ teaspoon garlic powder

In a large bowl, place spinach and lettuce, green onions, mandarin oranges, pine nuts, almonds, sunflower seed, and chicken. Mix dressing ingredients to combine thoroughly. Toss salad with desired amount of dressing just before serving.

Variation

Omit the chicken and use as a delightful Asian green salad side dish.

Sides

Au Gratin Potatoes

Watch out—these go quickly!

24 oz. frozen hash browns (cubed), thawed
2 cans (10.75 oz. each) cream of chicken soup
2 cups sour cream
1 ½ cups cheddar cheese, shredded and divided
½ cup butter, melted
⅓ cup onion, finely chopped
2 cups crushed cornflakes, bread crumbs, *or* crumbled potato chips
4 tablespoons butter, melted (omit if using potato chips)

Preheat oven to 350°F. Mix hash browns, cream of chicken soup, sour cream, 1 cup cheddar cheese, butter, and onion. Pour into a greased 9 x 13-inch pan. Sprinkle ½ cup cheddar cheese on top.

For topping, mix crushed cornflakes or bread crumbs with butter. (If using crumbled potato chips, omit butter.) Sprinkle topping over cheese.

Bake for 30 minutes. Serves 8 to 10.

Dill Potatoes

Easy to make, these potatoes go with almost any entrée.

8 medium red potatoes
2 tablespoons oil
¼ cup butter
3 garlic cloves, minced
1 teaspoon dried dill
½ teaspoon celery salt
¼ teaspoon salt
pepper to taste

Place potatoes in a steamer basket set over large saucepan filled with boiling water to a depth of about ¼ inch. Steam potatoes over medium-high heat, covered, until they are tender when pierced with the tip a knife, 10 to 15 minutes.

Cut cooked potatoes into quarters. Heat oil and melt butter in a large frying pan over medium heat, and sauté garlic in butter for 1 minute. Watch carefully so garlic won't burn. Add dill, celery salt, salt, and pepper to pan, then add potatoes and toss gently.

Serve immediately. Serves 4.

Golden Scalloped Potatoes

A healthier alternative without sacrificing flavor.

2 tablespoons butter or margarine
1 medium, onion, thinly sliced
1 cup milk
2 ½ cups chicken or vegetable broth
1 bay leaf
¼ teaspoon marjoram
¼ teaspoon thyme leaves
salt and pepper to taste
8 medium red potatoes, peeled and thinly
  sliced
½ cup shredded Monterey Jack cheese
¼ cup Parmesan cheese, grated

Preheat oven to 375°F. In a large saucepan, melt butter over medium heat. Add onion slices and sauté, stirring occasionally, until tender, about 7 minutes. Add milk, broth, bay leaf, marjoram, and thyme. Bring to a simmer and reduce liquid to about 3 cups, about 7 minutes. Remove bay leaf and season with salt and pepper to taste.

Add potato slices to liquid. Bring to a simmer and cook, stirring occasionally, for 5 minutes.

In a greased 9 x 13-inch baking pan, pour simmered potatoes. Bake 45 minutes. Top evenly with cheeses. Continue baking for 15 minutes or until cheese is melted, and casserole is bubbling. Let rest 5 minutes before serving. Serves 8.

Herbed Brown Rice

Delicious and savory!

1 can (14 oz.) chicken broth
1 ⅓ cups water
2 tablespoons butter
1 tablespoon dried onion
1 teaspoon dried parsley
¼ teaspoon garlic powder
¼ teaspoon ground thyme
⅛ teaspoon pepper
1 bay leaf
1 ⅓ cups uncooked brown rice

Add all ingredients, except brown rice, to saucepan and bring to a boil over medium high heat. Add rice and return to boil. Turn to low, cover, and simmer for 45 minutes. Remove bay leaf. Serve.

Don't have a fresh onion? Did you know that you can purchase frozen chopped onion in the frozen section at most grocery stores? It's great to have on hand when you find yourself without a fresh onion or you need to save an extra minute. Or, chop a few onions ahead of time and seal, label, and freeze for future use.

Herbed Quinoa Pilaf

The toasted almonds add a chewy texture and nutty flavor to this pilaf.

1 cup quinoa, rinsed and drained
1 tablespoon dried minced onion
¼ teaspoon dried basil
½ teaspoon salt
1 ½ cups water
1 tablespoon lemon juice
1 tablespoon vegetable oil
¼ cup slivered almonds, toasted or pine nuts

In a saucepan, combine quinoa, dried onion, basil, salt, and water. Bring to a boil. Reduce heat to low, cover, and simmer about 10 to 15 minutes, or until water is absorbed. Fluff with a fork. Stir in lemon juice, oil, and almonds. Serve immediately. Serves 6.

Barley Casserole

¼ cup butter
1 onion, chopped
1 can (4 oz.) sliced mushrooms
1 ½ cups pearl barley
1 can consommé soup plus water to equal 2 cups
1 tablespoon dried parsley

Preheat oven to 350°F. Saute onions, mushrooms, and barley in butter until onion is clear. Place all ingredients in a greased 9 x 13-inch baking dish. Cover with foil and bake for 50 minutes.

Quinoa

Quinoa (KEEN-wah) is an excellent source of calcium and protein. One cup of quinoa has as much calcium and protein as a quart of milk. Nutritionally, it's a powerhouse, as quinoa contains all the essential amino acids, plus iron and magnesium. Quinoa needs to be rinsed thoroughly; just place in a strainer and rinse with cool water.

Quinoa makes a nice side dish to serve with chicken, meats, or seafood. Leftover quinoa makes an excellent salad the next day. Add your favorite diced veggies and toss with a vinaigrette or your favorite salsa. Serve cold. Try adding beans (rinsed and drained), corn, peppers, onions (red or green), jicama, fresh tomatoes, or carrots.

Quinoa was a staple of the ancient Incas. Its delicate flavor makes it a great alternative to rice or couscous as a side dish.

Green Beans in Butter Sauce

Easy to make, these beans compliment almost any meal.

    1 lb. frozen green beans
    2 tablespoons butter or margarine
    1 teaspoon lemon juice or vinegar
    1 teaspoon Worcestershire sauce
    pepper to taste

In a large saucepan, add green beans and ⅓ cup water. Cover and cook for 7 to 9 minutes or until tender. Drain. Return to saucepan; add remaining ingredients. Stir until butter melts and sauce coats beans. Serve immediately. Serves 4.

Honey Butter Carrots

    1 lb. baby carrots
    2 tablespoons butter or margarine
    2 tablespoons honey
    salt and freshly ground pepper to taste
    1 teaspoon dried parsley

Place carrots on steamer rack over gently boiling water, cover, and steam for 12 to 15 minutes or until tender.

In a skillet over medium heat, melt butter with honey. Add carrots and salt and pepper. Mix well.

Sauté for 2 minutes. Transfer to a bowl and sprinkle with parsley. Serve immediately. Serves 4.

Variation

For a new flavor, add ¼ teaspoon ground ginger to melted butter and honey.

Maple Glazed Carrots

These sweet, buttery carrots are an amazing side dish. Even kids will like them.

    2 lbs. baby carrots or carrots cut lengthwise
       into 3-inch strips
    4 tablespoons butter or margarine
    1 clove garlic, halved
    4 tablespoons maple syrup
    salt and pepper to taste
    1 tablespoon dried parsley

In a saucepan, in boiling, salted water, cook carrots 8 to 10 minutes, until tender. Drain and set aside.

In a large skillet, melt butter or margarine over medium heat. Add garlic, sauté 2 minutes. Remove garlic; add syrup. Stir to combine. Add carrots and salt and pepper and sauté over medium-high heat 10 minutes or until lightly browned, stirring occasionally. Sprinkle with parsley and serve immediately. Serves 6.

Orzo Pilaf

A delicious change of pace from potatoes or rice.

1 tablespoon butter or margarine
4 green onions, sliced
1 garlic clove, minced
1 cup orzo
2 cups chicken broth
⅓ cup Parmesan cheese, grated
1 teaspoon dried parsley
salt and freshly ground pepper to taste

In a saucepan over medium heat melt butter. Add onion and garlic and sauté until vegetables are soft, about 5 minutes. Stir in orzo. Add chicken broth and bring to a boil. Reduce heat to low and cook, covered, until liquid is absorbed, 20 to 25 minutes.

Add cheese, parsley, and salt and pepper. Cook until cheese is melted, stirring once, about 5 minutes longer. Serve immediately. Serves 4 to 6.

Spanish Rice

This version of rice is a great accompaniment to enchiladas.

2 tablespoons vegetable oil
1 small green pepper, chopped
1 small onion, chopped
1 clove garlic, chopped
1 cup white rice
1 can (14.5 oz.) diced tomatoes
1 cup chicken broth
½ teaspoon cumin
¼ teaspoon salt
pepper to taste
1 teaspoon dried parsley

Heat oil in a saucepan over medium heat; add green pepper, onion, and garlic and sauté until tender, about 5 minutes. Add rice, tomatoes, broth, cumin, salt, and pepper; bring to a boil. Reduce heat to low and cook covered, 15 minutes, or until rice is tender. Turn off heat, let stand covered 5 minutes. Fluff with a fork. Sprinkle with parsley and serve. Serves 4.

Multi-Grain Pilaf

A flavorful and crunchy side dish.

 2 tablespoons oil
 ¾ cup white basmati rice
 ¾ cup quinoa, rinsed and drained
 3 cups chicken or vegetable broth
 ¼ teaspoon salt
 ¼ teaspoon pepper
 ½ cup dried cranberries, or chopped dried
 apricots
 ¾ cup pine nuts or chopped pistachio nuts

In a large saucepan, heat oil over medium heat, add rice and quinoa, and toast 1 to 2 minutes.

Add broth, salt, and pepper and bring to boil. Reduce heat to low and simmer 15 to 20 minutes or until liquid is absorbed. Add dried cranberries, and half of nuts, and fluff with fork. Sprinkle top with other half of nuts. Serve immediately. Serves 6.

Did you know? Basmati rice is known for its fragrant aroma (popcorn-like), and its nutlike flavor.

Mashed Sweet Potatoes with Maple Syrup

 1 can (29 oz.) sweet potatoes
 2 tablespoons butter
 2 tablespoons pure maple syrup (or brown
 sugar)
 ¼ teaspoon salt
 ¼ teaspoon pepper
 dash cinnamon (optional)

Pour sweet potatoes with liquid into a saucepan. Heat on medium until liquid is rapidly simmering and sweet potatoes are hot. Drain liquid and transfer sweet potatoes to a mixing bowl. Add butter, maple syrup, salt, pepper, and cinnamon. Beat with hand mixer until well blended and fluffy. Serve hot.

Note: This recipe could easily be done with fresh sweet potatoes. Wash two large sweet potatoes and cut into chunks. Boil in large saucepan with plenty of water until soft and tender. Drain water and transfer sweet potatoes to a mixing bowl. Because canned sweet potatoes are packed in light syrup, you will need to add more maple syrup or brown sugar if using fresh. Follow directions above and enjoy.

Perfect Brown Rice

2¼ cups water
1 tablespoon olive oil
1 cup brown rice
1 teaspoon chicken bouillon

Bring water and olive oil to a boil. Add brown rice and chicken bouillon. Bring to boil, cover, turn to low. Let cook 45 minutes. Fluff with fork.

Note: You can also place all ingredients in a rice cooker and cook according to directions for brown rice.

Neon Rice

Turmeric adds a lovely yellow color to this rice and is a healthy antioxidant.

2 tablespoons oil
¾ cup white basmati rice
1 small onion, diced
1 garlic clove
¾ teaspoon ground turmeric
1½ cups chicken broth
¼ teaspoon salt

In a saucepan, heat oil over medium heat. Add rice, onion, garlic, and turmeric. Cook, stirring constantly, until onion is tender. Add chicken broth and salt. Cover and simmer about 15 minutes or until liquid is absorbed. Fluff with fork and serve. Serves 4.

Quinoa and Carrot Pilaf

A great way to add whole grains to your diet.

2 tablespoons vegetable oil
1 small onion, chopped
2 garlic cloves, minced
½ cup chopped carrot
1 cup quinoa, rinsed and drained
¼ cup water
1 can (14 oz.) chicken broth
¼ teaspoon thyme
salt and pepper to taste

In a saucepan heat oil over medium heat. Add onion, garlic and carrot; sauté stirring frequently until soft, about 5 minutes. Stir in quinoa, water, chicken broth, thyme, salt and pepper. Bring to a boil. Reduce heat to low, cover and simmer until all liquid is absorbed, about 10 to 13 minutes. Let stand 5 minutes. Fluff with fork. Serves 4.

Sweet Potato Fries

Even the pickiest eater will love these fries.

2 large sweet potatoes
2 to 3 tablespoons olive oil
1 ½ teaspoons seasoned salt

Preheat oven to 425°F. Wash sweet potatoes and cut into strips or semi rounds (leave skins on). In a large bowl, toss cut sweet potatoes with olive oil and seasoned salt. Transfer to a lightly greased jelly roll pan and bake for 45 minutes or until light brown and crispy. Stir once or twice during baking. Baking time will vary depending on thickness of the potato slices.

Dipping Sauce

The perfect complement to Sweet Potato Fries.

¼ cup applesauce
¼ cup apricot jam

Mix together in a small dish and serve with Sweet Potato Fries.

Nutrition Tip: Sweet potatoes are packed with heart healthy and cancer fighting nutrients. These flavorful orange spuds are rich in antioxidants, such as beta-carotene, loaded with vitamin C and potassium, and full of fiber.

Roasted Sweet Potatoes and Onions

A wonderful combination of flavors.

2 medium onions, coarsely chopped
3 large or 4 medium sweet potatoes, cut into 3-inch pieces
¼ to ⅓ cup vegetable oil (enough to coat sweet potatoes)
½ teaspoon garlic powder
½ teaspoon salt
¼ teaspoon pepper

Preheat oven to 425°F. In a large bowl, toss ingredients well, making sure sweet potatoes are coated with oil. Place in a 9 x 13-inch baking dish. Bake for 40 to 45 minutes or until tender, stirring every 10 minutes to ensure even cooking.

Use the french-fry slicer on your food processor to make Sweet Potato Fries if you have one.

Tortilla Chip Dip

Ole!

- 1 ½ cups of dehydrated refried beans *or* 2 cans (16 oz. each) refried beans
- 1 cup salsa
- 1 cup sour cream
- 1 package (1.25 oz.) dry taco seasoning (about 5 tablespoons)
- 2 cups guacamole dip
- 2 cups cheddar or Monterey Jack cheese, shredded
- 3 medium tomatoes, seeded, coarsely chopped
- 1 bunch green onions, chopped
- 1 can (4.25 oz.) chopped black olives
- tortilla chips

Prepare dehydrated refried beans according to package directions. Mix the beans and salsa together. Spread onto a large serving platter.

Combine sour cream and taco seasoning. Spread onto the refried bean layer.

Top with guacamole dip, cheese, chopped tomatoes, green onions, and black olives.

Serve chilled or at room temperature with tortilla chips. Serves 15.

Toasted Crumb Topper

Top cooked green vegetables, potatoes, or pasta with these crunchy crumbs.

- 2 cups coarse fresh bread crumbs from whole wheat, French, or sourdough bread
- ¼ cup vegetable oil
- ½ teaspoon salt

Spread bread crumbs evenly in a jelly roll pan lightly coated with cooking spray. Bake at 350°F for about 10 to 15 minutes or until golden. Transfer to a mixing bowl, toss with oil and salt.

Snacks

Peanut Butter Balls

Watch out Reese's!

1 cup powdered sugar
1 cup peanut butter
½ cup instant powdered milk
3 tablespoons water
30 Hershey's Kisses

Combine powdered sugar, peanut butter, powdered milk, and water. Shape into 1" balls. Press an unwrapped chocolate kiss into the center of each peanut butter ball. Arrange on cookie sheet and refrigerate until firm, about 20 minutes.

Variation

Omit chocolate kiss and roll peanut butter balls in finely crushed graham cracker crumbs. May also dip one half of peanut butter ball in melted chocolate (refrigerate before dipping and after dipping). Try white chocolate, too.

Caramel Corn

The real thing—crunchy, sweet, and out of this world.

12 cups popped corn (about ½ cup unpopped corn)
1 cup butter or margarine
2 cups brown sugar, packed
¼ cup corn syrup
1 teaspoon salt
2 teaspoons vanilla
½ teaspoon baking soda
1 cup peanuts, almonds, or pecans (optional)

Preheat oven to 250°F. In a large bowl, place popcorn, set aside. In a large saucepan, over medium-low heat, combine butter, brown sugar, corn syrup, and salt. Bring to a boil, stirring constantly. Boil for 5 minutes, stirring frequently. Remove from heat. With long spoon, stir in vanilla and baking soda (can bubble so be careful not to get burned).

Quickly pour syrup over popped corn and stir until coated well. Spread in a jelly roll pan with sides. Bake for 45 minutes, stirring every 15 minutes, stirring in nuts after 30 minutes. Turn out onto waxed paper. Cool completely. Store in airtight container.

Chewy Granola Bars

A favorite with the kids.

½ cup butter or margarine, softened
1 cup brown sugar, packed
¼ cup sugar
1 teaspoon vanilla
1 egg
1 cup flour
1 teaspoon cinnamon
½ teaspoon baking powder
¼ teaspoon salt
1¼ cups crisp rice cereal
1½ cups quick oats
1 cup dried cranberries (or craisins)
½ cup white chocolate chips
½ cup finely chopped pecans or walnuts
  (optional)

Preheat oven to 350°F. Cream butter and sugars. Add vanilla and egg and mix well. Add flour, cinnamon, baking powder, salt, crisp rice cereal, and oats to creamed mixture and mix to blend. Fold in cranberries, chocolate chips, and nuts. Press into a greased 9 x 13-inch pan. Bake for 25 minutes.

Cut into squares and wrap individually with plastic wrap. Makes for a fun lunch treat or an "on-the-go" snack.

Variation

Even though our favorite was the dried cranberries and white chocolate chips, a delicious variation is to use raisins and semisweet chocolate chips.

Classic Granola

Sure to please the young and the not-so-young.

4 cups rolled oats
1 cup sliced almonds
½ cup brown sugar
½ teaspoon salt
2 teaspoons cinnamon
¼ cup honey
¼ cup oil
1 teaspoon vanilla
1 cup raisins
1 cup dehydrated apples, or other dried fruit,
  cut up (optional)

Preheat oven to 300°F. In a bowl, mix oats, almonds, brown sugar, salt, and cinnamon. In a saucepan, warm the honey and oil and stir in vanilla. Carefully pour liquid over oat mixture and gently stir. Spread granola on a jelly roll pan and bake 30 to 40 minutes, stirring every 10 minutes. Add raisins and apples during last 5 minutes of baking. Transfer pan to a rack and cool. Store in an airtight container at room temperature.

Peanut Butter Candy
So easy and good.

½ cup peanut butter
½ cup honey
1 cup powdered milk
¼ cup powdered sugar, sifted

Combine peanut butter and honey in a mixing
bowl. Add powdered milk and powdered sugar
a little at a time until thoroughly mixed (I like to
knead the dough with my hands). Roll into balls.
Store in an air tight container in refrigerator.

Variation
Add ¼ cup flaked coconut to dough before
rolling into balls. Or drizzle snacks with melted
chocolate and chill.

Crunchy Apple Wedges
A fun snack that is both pleasing and nutritious.

2 apples, cored, sliced into wedges
1 cup rice square cereal, crushed
1 tablespoon brown sugar
3 to 4 tablespoons peanut butter, creamy or
  crunchy

Pat apple wedges dry with paper towels. In a
shallow bowl, stir together crushed cereal and
brown sugar. Spread peanut butter on cut sides
of apple wedges and press into cereal mixture
until evenly coated. Serve immediately.

Crispy Rice Treats
A special treat that's a snap to make.

½ cup chopped peanuts or cashews or favorite
  nut
2 cups crispy rice cereal
½ teaspoon cinnamon
½ cup corn syrup
¾ cup peanut butter
½ teaspoon vanilla

In a large bowl, combine peanuts, rice cereal,
and cinnamon. Set aside. In a saucepan, over
medium heat bring corn syrup to a boil. Reduce
heat to low and simmer 2 minutes. Stir in peanut
butter and cook 2 to 3 minutes. Remove from
heat, add vanilla. Stir peanut butter mixture
into cereal mixture until coated. Spoon into a
greased 8-inch pan, pressing evenly. Cool, cut
into squares.

Maple Nut Granola

4 cups rolled oats
1 cup chopped walnuts or pecans
1 cup coconut
1 cup sliced or slivered almonds
¼ cup sunflower seeds
¼ cup sesame seeds
½ teaspoon salt
¼ cup brown sugar
2 teaspoons cinnamon
½ teaspoon ground cloves
1 cup oil
½ cup honey
¼ cup pure maple syrup

2 cups dried fruit (any combination of raisins, cranberries, cherries, or apples)

Preheat oven to 325°F. In a large bowl combine oats, walnuts, coconut, almonds, sunflower seeds, sesame seeds, salt, brown sugar, cinnamon, and cloves. In a small saucepan, mix oil, honey, and maple syrup. Heat until honey has melted and is combined thoroughly. Stir into dry mixture. Spread on a greased 15 x 10-inch jelly roll pan and bake for 30 to 40 minutes, stirring every 10 minutes during baking. Remove and add choice of dried fruits. Stir several times during cooling process to keep granola from sticking together. Store in airtight container.

Partially Hydrogenated Oil

We should all try to avoid foods containing partially hydrogenated oil (also known as trans fat). Trans fats seem to have made their way into almost every processed food from cookies to margarine.

Always check the nutrition label and the ingredient list. Quite often, nutrition labels will state "O grams of trans fat" yet "partially hydrogenated oil" will be listed in the ingredients. The federal guidelines say that if the trans fat content is less than .5 grams per serving, it can be listed as "o grams per serving" on the label even though technically, trans fats are in the product. Many food manufacturers are reformulating their products to eliminate trans fat completely and there are great margarines, shortenings, biscuit mixes and other products on the market that are truly trans fat free. Again, check the labels and list of ingredients carefully to make a wise nutritional choice for your family.

Yogurt Orange Cream Pops

A dreamy, creamy frozen treat.

> 1 quart (4 cups) plain or vanilla yogurt
> ⅔ cup water
> ⅔ cup powdered milk
> 1 can (12 oz.) frozen orange juice concentrate
> 1 teaspoon vanilla

Combine all ingredients in blender and mix thoroughly. Pour into 2 oz. paper cups, put a popsicle stick in each, and freeze at least 3 hours. Peel away the paper cup and enjoy. Makes 15 to 20 servings.

We love this treat because it is naturally sweetened with fruit juice concentrate. However, if you prefer it to taste more like the sweetened store-bought treats, add ¼ cup sugar and reduce yogurt to 3 cups.

Variation

Try different frozen juice concentrates for your family's favorite fun flavor.

Fudge Pops

> 4 cups water
> ¾ cup sugar
> 1 tablespoon cornstarch
> ½ cup cocoa powder
> 3 tablespoons flour
> ¼ teaspoon salt
> 1 ¼ cups powdered milk
> 1 teaspoon vanilla

In medium saucepan, bring 4 cups of water to a boil. Mix dry ingredients in a bowl and add all at once to boiling water. Boil for 1 minute, stirring constantly. Add vanilla. Pour into 2 oz. paper cups, put a popsicle stick in each, and freeze at least 3 hours. Peel away the paper cup and enjoy.

Soups

Black Bean Soup

Tasty and full of flavor, a great appetizer soup.

1 onion, chopped
2 to 3 green onions, trimmed and chopped
1 tablespoon olive oil
2 garlic cloves, minced
½ teaspoon ground cumin
1 teaspoon dried oregano
2 cans (15.5 oz. each) black beans, undrained
2 cups water
¼ teaspoon red pepper flakes
¼ teaspoon salt
¼ teaspoon pepper
1 bay leaf
½ cup orange juice
sour cream and sprig of cilantro for garnish

In a large saucepan, sauté onion and green onion in olive oil over medium-high heat until soft and clear, about 3 minutes. Add garlic, cumin, and oregano and sauté for another minute. Add beans, water, red pepper flakes, salt, pepper, and bay leaf. Bring the soup to a boil. Reduce heat and simmer, uncovered, for 20 minutes. Stir in the orange juice. Cook for another 5 minutes. Discard bay leaf.

Ladle ½ of the soup into a blender or food processor and puree. Return pureed mixture to saucepan and stir to combine. The soup should contain whole beans and onions as well as the pureed liquid. Serve hot. Garnish each bowl with a dollop of sour cream and a sprig of cilantro. Serves 4.

Note: For a spicier soup, increase red pepper flakes to ½ teaspoon and cumin to 1 teaspoon

Chicken Tortilla Soup

It's so easy to make, and because you don't have to cook it for long, it's fast to the table. Vary the heat by the type of salsa you use.

2 cans (10.5 oz. each) chicken with rice soup
1 cup mild to medium chunky salsa
½ cup water
1 can (15 oz.) chili beans
1 can (15 oz.) whole kernel corn, drained
1 can (12 oz.) canned chicken breast
1 teaspoon cumin
½ teaspoon chili powder

Topping

tortilla chips
shredded cheese
sour cream

In a large saucepan, combine all ingredients except toppings. Bring to a boil, reduce heat to medium and simmer for 5 minutes. Serve topped

with chips, cheese, and a dollop of sour cream.
Serves 4.

Grandma's Chili

An oldie but goodie.

1 lb. ground beef
1 onion, chopped
1 green pepper, chopped
1 cup carrots, chopped
1 cup celery, chopped
1 can (14.5 oz.) ready-cut tomatoes
1 can (12 oz.) tomato juice or V-8 juice
2 tablespoons brown sugar
2 tablespoons vinegar
1 teaspoon chili powder
1 ½ teaspoons salt
dash garlic powder
2 cans (15 oz. each) kidney beans or small
   red beans, and drained

Brown ground beef and onions until meat is no
longer pink. Drain. Add vegetables and remaining ingredients and cook until steaming freely.
Simmer on low with lid on for 2 hours. This is a
good recipe to double. Serves 6.

Corn Chowder

You can substitute vegetable broth for the chicken
broth and omit the bacon for a vegetarian alternative.

1 tablespoon vegetable oil
1 small onion, chopped
1 small green pepper, chopped
1 can (15 oz.) whole kernel corn, drained
1 can (16 oz.) cream of corn
2 cans (14 oz. each) chicken broth
¾ cup heavy cream
½ teaspoon dried thyme
salt and pepper to taste
cooked, crumbled bacon (optional)

In a saucepan, heat oil over medium heat. Add
onion and green pepper, cook until soft.

Add corn, cream of corn, broth, cream, thyme,
and salt and pepper. Bring to a gentle boil,
reduce heat to medium and simmer 5 minutes.
Top each serving with crumbled bacon if desired.
Serves 4 to 6.

Creamy Potato Soup

8 slices bacon, cut into 1-inch pieces or pre-cooked bacon
5 large potatoes (about 4 lbs)
1 large onion, chopped
3 teaspoons salt or to taste
2 tablespoons cornstarch
1 cup sour cream
½ cup butter or margarine
2⅔ cups milk
½ teaspoon black pepper
½ teaspoon garlic powder
5 green onions, thinly sliced
1 cup shredded sharp cheddar cheese
chicken broth, if soup needs to be thinned

Cook the bacon pieces over medium heat in a large skillet until crisp. Transfer bacon to paper towel to drain and set aside. Peel, rinse, and cut the potatoes into thirds. Place potatoes and chopped onion in a large pot with water to cover, add 2 teaspoons salt, and bring to a boil. Reduce heat to a simmer and cook until the potatoes are very soft—about 45 minutes. Drain the potatoes and onions, discarding the water, and return them to the pot. Mash them with a potato masher until smooth. Add the sour cream and butter and stir until melted. Add cornstarch to ¼ cup of the milk. Stir until cornstarch is dissolved. Add cornstarch mixture, the remaining milk, pepper, remaining salt to taste, and garlic powder. Bring the soup back to a simmer and cook until slightly thickened, about 5 to 10 minutes, stirring occasionally. Serve topped with green onions and cheese. Serves 8.

For a chunkier version, add one potato cut up in chunks and cooked until knife pierces easily.

For a great presentation, serve soup in a hollowed out Bread Bowl Variation (p. 42).

Taco Soup

1 lb. ground beef
1 onion, chopped
2 cans (15 oz. each) diced tomatoes with juice
2 cans (15 oz. each) canned kidney beans, drained
1 can (16 oz.) tomato juice or V-8 juice
1 can (16 oz.) canned corn, drained
1 package (1.25 oz.) dry taco seasoning (5 tablespoons)
garnish with corn chips, grated cheese, and sour cream

Sauté ground beef and onion in stockpot over medium heat until beef is cooked through and onion is tender. Add the remaining ingredients and simmer 20 to 30 minutes. Serve hot and garnish with corn chips, grated cheese, and sour cream.

Creamy Tomato Soup

3 small green onions
1 can (14.5 oz.) diced tomatoes
1 cup chicken broth
¼ cup milk
1 teaspoon sugar
½ teaspoon salt
salt and pepper to taste
dash of celery salt
¼ cup whipping cream (optional)
Parmesan cheese, grated
dried basil

Peel away the outer layer of skin from green onions. Cut the white part of the onion and about 2 inches of the green into slices and put in blender. Add to the blender canned tomatoes, broth, milk, sugar, and salt. Blend until very smooth (1 to 2 minutes). Pour into a medium saucepan and set over medium high heat. Bring the soup to a boil, reduce heat to low and simmer, stirring frequently until the soup thickens, about 15 minutes. You should have about 2½ cups of soup. Add salt, pepper, and a dash of celery salt to taste. Remove from heat and add cream. Stir to blend. Ladle soup into bowls and sprinkle with Parmesan cheese and dried basil. Top with Garlic Croutons (p. 133) if desired. Serve immediately.

Hamburger Soup

A great main course soup.

1 lb. ground beef or turkey
3 cups water
1 can (14 oz.) chicken broth
1 can (15 oz.) corn, drained
1 can (8 oz.) tomato sauce
¼ cup ketchup
1 tablespoon soy sauce
1 cup sliced carrots
1 cup sliced celery
1 envelope dry onion soup mix
½ teaspoon seasoned salt
1 bay leaf
½ teaspoon basil
½ teaspoon oregano
pepper to taste
1 cup small shaped pasta, cooked

In a large stockpot, cook ground beef or turkey until no longer pink. Add water, chicken broth, corn, tomato sauce, ketchup, soy sauce, carrots, celery, dried onion soup mix, seasoned salt, bay leaf, basil, oregano, and pepper to taste. Bring to a boil. Reduce heat to low, simmer 50 to 60 minutes. Remove bay leaf. Stir in cooked pasta. Serve.

Pantry Bean Soup
Hearty and delicious.

2 cans (14 oz. each) chicken broth
1 cup water
16 oz. of your favorite frozen vegetable mix
 (try stir fry veggies)
1 can (14.5 oz.) diced tomatoes
⅓ cup elbow macaroni
1 can (15 oz.) black beans, drained
1 can (15 oz.) white beans, drained

1 teaspoon Italian seasoning
½ teaspoon garlic powder
¼ teaspoon pepper
¼ cup Parmesan cheese

In a stockpot over medium-high heat, add chicken broth, water, vegetables and canned tomatoes. Cover and bring to a boil. Add pasta, beans, Italian seasoning, garlic powder, and pepper and continue to boil for 10 minutes, stirring frequently, until pasta is tender. Add Parmesan cheese and simmer a few minutes before serving. Serves 6.

Using Dry Beans in Cooking

Quick Soak Method: Place dry beans in a saucepan and cover with water. Bring to a boil (add 1 tablespoon of oil to prevent excessive foaming), then remove from heat. Cover and let sit 60 to 90 minutes. Drain and rinse.

Overnight Soak Method: For each cup of dry beans, dissolve 1 teaspoon salt in 3 cups of water. Add beans and let stand over night. Drain and rinse.

Cooking Beans: Once beans have been rehydrated, they need to be cooked. Always discard soaking water. To cook rehydrated beans, place beans in a saucepan and cover with 2 to 3 inches of fresh water. Bring to a boil and then simmer covered for 3 to 4 hours. Drain and rinse. Use in recipes as called for. Soaked beans (drained and rinsed) can be transferred directly to soups for cooking if the soup simmers for at least 3 to 4 hours.

Freezing Beans: You can store cooked beans in the freezer for many, many, months (even years!). Soak and cook a large pot of beans and then seal them in bags. Label and freeze for convenient future use. Freeze soaked and cooked beans in quantities of 1 ½ cups, which equals one 15 oz. can. Thaw and use in recipes and usual.

Three-Bean Chili

This hearty soup is a great way to use pantry items.

1 cup onion, chopped
1 garlic clove, chopped
2 tablespoons oil
1 can (15 oz.) tomato sauce
1 can (14.5 oz.) diced tomatoes
1 can (15 oz.) black beans, rinsed and drained
1 can (15 oz.) white beans, rinsed and drained
1 can (15 oz.) kidney beans, rinsed and drained
1 can (4 .25 oz.) diced green chilies
1 package chili seasoning mix
½ cup ketchup
1 cup chicken broth
cooked rice or pasta (optional)
mozzarella cheese

In a large saucepan, over medium heat, add onion and garlic. Cook, stirring, for 5 minutes or until tender. Add tomato sauce, tomatoes, beans, chilies, seasoning, ketchup, and broth. Bring to a boil; reduce heat to low. Simmer covered for 25 minutes, stirring occasionally. Ladle into bowls over rice or pasta and top with cheese.

To make this recipe completely from food storage items, substitute 2 tablespoons dry onions for fresh onion and ½ teaspoon garlic powder for garlic clove. Add with all ingredients (skip step to cook onions and garlic in saucepan until tender). Serves 6.

Pinto Bean Soup

Surprisingly fabulous!

1 tablespoon oil
1 onion, chopped
1 rib celery, chopped
2 cans (15 oz. each) pinto beans, rinsed and drained
1 can (14.5 oz.) diced tomatoes
¼ teaspoon salt
¼ teaspoon pepper
1 bay leaf
1 can chicken broth
grated cheddar cheese
sour cream

In a large saucepan over medium heat, combine olive oil, onion, and celery and cook until soft. Add pinto beans, tomatoes, salt, pepper, bay leaf, and chicken broth. Bring to a boil, then reduce heat and simmer, covered, for 20 minutes.

Remove from heat and discard bay leaf. Ladle half of soup into blender or food processor and puree until smooth. Return pureed mixture to soup. The soup should contain whole beans and chopped onions as well as the smooth pureed mixture. Garnish each bowl with a sprinkling of grated cheddar cheese and a dollop of sour cream.

White Bean-Chicken Chili

Love chili, but ready for a change of pace? Try this delicious white chili version.

2 tablespoons vegetable oil
1 large onion, chopped
4 cloves garlic, minced
3 cans (14 oz. each) chicken broth
3 cans (15 oz. each) great northern beans, rinsed and drained
4 cups chicken (uncooked), chopped
1 can (4 oz.) chopped green chillies
1½ to 2 tablespoons cumin
1 teaspoon chili powder
2 teaspoons oregano
¼ teaspoon cayenne pepper
2 cups jack cheese, grated
1 cup sour cream

Toppings

shredded jack cheese, chopped tomatoes, avocado, and fresh cilantro, if desired

Heat oil in a large stockpot over medium-low heat; add onion and garlic. Cook, stirring frequently, until onion is tender.

Add chicken broth, beans, and chopped chicken, simmer 10 minutes. Stir in chilies, cumin, chili powder, oregano, and cayenne pepper. Bring to boil and simmer 20 minutes more, stirring occasionally. Stir in sour cream and cheese before serving.

Top white bean chili with more shredded jack cheese, chopped tomatoes, chopped avocado, and chopped fresh cilantro, if desired. Serves 6 to 8.

Split Pea Soup

Rich and smooth, this soup warms up any chilly day.

8 cups cold water
1 lb. split peas, rinsed (about 2¼ cups)
1½ lb. ham bone
1 teaspoon chicken bouillon
1 onion, diced
1 bay leaf
¼ teaspoon pepper
¼ teaspoon ground marjoram
2 medium carrots, chopped
2 stalks celery, chopped

In a stockpot, add water, split peas, ham bone, chicken bouillon, onion, bay leaf, pepper, and marjoram and bring to a boil. Reduce heat and simmer for one hour, stirring occasionally. Take ham bone out, cut off excess meat and then add meat back to soup with carrots and celery. Bring to a boil and then reduce heat and simmer on low for 30 minutes. Remove bay leaf. Serve hot.

Chicken & Dumplings

A delicious comfort food.

Soup

    4 skinless, boneless chicken breasts
    1 cup celery, chopped
    1 cup carrots, chopped
    1 onion, diced
    2 teaspoons salt
    ½ teaspoon pepper
    2 teaspoons dried parsley or 2 tablespoons
      fresh parsley, minced
    2 teaspoons dried thyme
    ½ teaspoon dried rosemary

Dumplings

    1 cup white flour
    1 cup wheat flour
    1 teaspoon salt
    3 teaspoons baking powder
    2 teaspoons dried parsley or 2 tablespoons
      fresh parsley, minced
    ¼ cup butter or margarine
    ¾ cup milk

Place soup ingredients in a stockpot and add enough water to cover. Bring to a boil. Reduce heat and simmer for 20 minutes. While soup is simmering, make dumplings.

For dumplings, combine flours, salt, baking powder, and parsley in mixing bowl. Cut in butter with pastry cutter until dough looks like coarse crumbs. Stir in milk and mix with a fork just until dough is moistened and holds together. Gently roll dough into 2-inch balls with the palm of hands. Makes about 15 dumplings.

Take each chicken breast out of soup and chop with a knife and fork on a cutting board. Return chopped chicken to soup. Drop dumpling balls into the simmering broth. Cover and continue to simmer for 20 minutes without lifting the lid. To serve, ladle soup into soup bowls making sure each serving gets a couple of dumplings. Delicious! Serves 6.

Chilled Strawberry Soup

Completely refreshing, this soup makes a great springtime appetizer.

  8 cups whole strawberries, divided (2 to 2 ½ lbs.)
  ¼ cup sugar
  1 cup white grape juice
  ½ cup vanilla yogurt

Wash and hull strawberries. Reserve one cup of strawberries and set aside. Place remaining strawberries with sugar in blender or food processor and puree until smooth. Transfer to a bowl and stir in grape juice. Chill for two to three hours. Before serving, dice reserved cup of strawberries. To serve, ladle soup into soup bowls and top individual bowls with a dollop of vanilla yogurt and cut strawberries.

Chilled Tropical Fruit Soup: Top each bowl with a cut up fruit medley of strawberries, kiwi, and mango.

Chilled Strawberry Banana Soup: Top each bowl with cut strawberries and banana slices.

Chilled Patriotic Soup: Top each bowl with and cut strawberries, raspberries, and blueberries.

Substitutions & Such

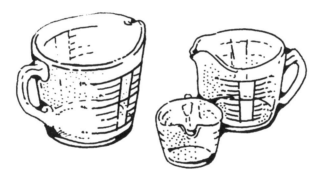

Substitutions

1 square unsweetened baking chocolate (1 ounce) = 3 tablespoons cocoa + 1 tablespoon oil

1 tablespoon cornstarch (for thickening) = 2 tablespoons flour

1 teaspoon baking powder = ¼ teaspoon baking soda + ½ teaspoon cream of tartar

1 cup buttermilk or sour milk = 1 cup fluid milk with 1 tablespoon vinegar or lemon juice stirred into it
(let stand 5 minutes)

1 tablespoon fresh herbs = 1 teaspoon dried herbs

1 tablespoon fresh mustard = 1 teaspoon dry mustard

1 small pressed garlic clove = ⅛ teaspoon garlic powder

1 small fresh onion = 2 tablespoons dried onion

2 medium bananas (approx.) = 1 cup mashed bananas

1 cup cream = ⅓ cup butter + ⅔ cup milk

1 cup fluid milk = ¼ cup powdered milk + 1 cup water

1 quart fluid milk = ⅔ cup powdered milk + 1 quart water (4 cups)

1 gallon fluid milk = 2⅔ cups powdered milk + 1 gallon water (16 cups)

1 cup white sugar = ¾ cup honey (reduce liquid by ¼ cup)

1 cup honey = 1 ¼ cups sugar (increase liquid by ¼ cup)

1 cup corn syrup = 1 cup sugar + ¼ cup liquid

1 cup brown sugar = 1 cup white sugar + 1 tablespoon molasses

Recipes for Basic Ingredients

Sweetened Condensed Milk

⅓ cup boiling water
2 tablespoons butter, softened
1 cup powdered milk
¾ cup sugar
½ teaspoon vanilla

Pour boiling water, butter, and powdered milk into a bowl and beat well with hand mixer. Gradually add sugar and vanilla, beating well. Store in refrigerator. Mixture will thicken slightly as it stands.

Equals one 14 oz. can of sweetened condensed milk.

Buttermilk

1 cup water
½ cup powdered milk
1 tablespoon vinegar or lemon juice

Mix and let stand 2 to 3 minutes.

Evaporated Milk

1 cup water
1 cup powdered milk

Mix to blend and use in recipes as you would one can of evaporated milk.

Note: This recipe is for a non-fat evaporated milk. For whole evaporated milk, add a small amount of butter (about ½ teaspoon).

Whipped Topping

½ cup ice water
½ cup powdered milk
½ cup powdered sugar
½ teaspoon vanilla

Combine ice water and milk in bowl beat on high for 10 minutes. Add powdered sugar and vanilla and continue to beat well until thoroughly blended. Chill. This works best in a stand mixer with whip beaters. If mixture begins to fall, you can always beat it again.

Mock Parmesan Cheese

1 cup water
1 cup powdered milk
3 tablespoons lemon juice
salt

Bring water to a boil in a saucepan. Add powdered milk and stir to dissolve. Add lemon juice and return mixture to a boil. Milk will look frothy with curds. Pour into a cloth-lined strainer (cheese cloth work very well) to catch curds. Gather up edges of cloth and rinse milk curds thoroughly, squeezing out excess water. Curds will be pressed into a ball of cheese-like substance. Place curds on a baking sheet and using your fingers break up into crumbly curds. Bake at 170°F (lowest temperature on oven) for 10 minutes. Lightly salt and transfer to an airtight container or sealed bag and refrigerate. Flavor increases as the curds age.

Mock Ricotta Cheese

2 cups water
1 ½ cups powdered milk
1 cup plain yogurt
½ teaspoon salt (to taste)

Bring water to a boil in a large saucepan. Remove from heat, add powdered milk, and stir to thoroughly dissolve. Heat milk to boiling. Stir in yogurt and again bring mixture to a boil. The milk will curdle. Boil for a few minutes. You will see the milk curdle and the liquid become clear "curds and whey." Remove from heat. Pour milk curds in to a cloth-lined strainer (cheese cloth works well). Rinse. Gather up edges of cloth and rinse milk curds thoroughly with cool water, squeezing out excess water. Break up curds with fingers and add salt to taste. Refrigerate in airtight container. Makes 1 ½ cups.

Condensed Cream Soup Mix

2 cups powdered milk
⅔ cup cornstarch
2 tablespoons dry onion soup mix
1 ½ tablespoons chicken bouillon
¼ teaspoon celery salt
¼ teaspoon pepper
¼ teaspoon garlic powder

Mix ingredients together and store in an air-tight container.

To use mix, add ⅔ cup of Condensed Cream Soup Mix and 1⅓ cups water in a small saucepan. Cook and stir until thick, about 3 to 4 minutes. Use in recipes in place of one can of commercial condensed soup. This makes a low fat soup. If regular soup is desired, stir in a pad of butter.

Yogurt Sour Cream
A delightfully light and refreshing substitute.

2 cups plain yogurt

Place yogurt into a cloth lined strainer. Cheese cloth works wonderfully. You could also use a coffee filter or paper towel. Place the strainer over a bowl and cover yogurt with a damp paper towel. Let sit in refrigerator for 6 to 10 hours. Yogurt will be thick and the consistency of sour cream. Use it in recipes just as you would sour cream.

Yogurt Cheese

Yogurt Sour Cream (from previous recipe)

Follow the directions for Yogurt Sour Cream. However, let yogurt sit in refrigerator for 24 to 48 hours. The result will be a nice thick, yet spreadable cheese, similar to that of cream cheese.

This new yogurt cheese can be dressed up with herbs and spices to make a delightful spread on pita bread, crackers or even used as a vegetable dip.

Herbed Yogurt Cheese

½ cup Yogurt Cheese
½ teaspoon basil
½ teaspoon Italian Seasoning
dash of salt
dash of pepper
dash of garlic powder

Season to taste and use as a spread on bread varieties. Top with julienne sun-dried tomatoes, chopped cucumber, green or red pepper, and/or other fresh veggies.

Fruit Yogurt Cheese

½ cup Yogurt Cheese
3 to 4 tablespoons of your favorite jam

Spread on a bagel. Pure heaven!

Yogurt Cheese Ball

1 cup Yogurt Cheese (p. 165)
1 cup grated, extra sharp cheddar cheese
1 tablespoon minced onion
1 tablespoon dried parsley
¼ teaspoon garlic powder
¼ teaspoon salt
¼ teaspoon pepper
½ cup chopped pecans

Combine yogurt cheese, cheddar cheese, and seasonings until well combined. Press mixture with palms of hands into a large ball. Roll in chopped pecans. Wrap tightly in plastic wrap and refrigerate. Serve with crackers and pretzels.

Yogurt Cottage Cheese

4 cups water
2 cups powdered milk
1 cup vinegar
¼ teaspoon salt

Heat water in a large saucepan over low heat and add powdered milk, stirring to dissolve. When milk is very hot but not boiling, slowly pour vinegar around the edge of pan and gently stir. Remove from heat. Continue to pour vinegar and gently stir. Milk will begin to curdle and form a ball in the middle of the pan. Let rest for 2 minutes. The liquid around the curd ball should be clear. If it is still milky add more vinegar and gently stir. The white cheese clump is called "curds" and the liquid is called "whey."

Line a strainer or colander with cheese cloth. Carefully pour the pan of curds into the strainer, letting the whey run through. Lightly rinse with cool water, breaking up curds with fingers to rinse thoroughly. Gather up edges of cloth and continue to rinse curds with cool water. Squeeze out excess water, removing as much moisture as you can. Transfer curds to a bowl and break up curds with fingers. Add about ¼ cup of yogurt or sour cream to "cream" the mixture and add salt to taste. Chill. Makes 1 ½ cups of cottage cheese.

Basic White Sauce

1 cup water
1 tablespoon butter
4 tablespoons flour
3 tablespoons powdered milk
1 teaspoon chicken bouillon granules
dash of pepper
¼ teaspoon onion salt

Bring water and butter to a boil. In a separate bowl, mix together flour, powdered milk, bouillon, pepper, and onion salt. Turn heat to low and slowly add dry ingredients to water stirring constantly with a wire whisk. Return to boil and continue beating while sauce cooks for one minute. As soon as it thickens, remove from heat. May thin with milk if desired.

Variations

Alfredo Sauce Variation: Add ½ cup Parmesan cheese and ½ teaspoon dried parsley.

Cheddar Sauce Variation: Add ½ cup grated cheddar cheese.

Taco Seasoning

2 teaspoons dried onion
1 teaspoon paprika
1 teaspoon chili powder
½ teaspoon garlic powder
½ teaspoon crushed red pepper
¼ teaspoon dried oregano leaves
½ teaspoon cumin
½ teaspoon cornstarch
½ teaspoon salt

Mix all ingredients together. May put mixture in a nut and seed grinder to grind to a fine powder.

This mixture will be lighter in color than commercial taco seasoning because of the cornstarch but will be very similar in flavor.

Tomato Ketchup

2 cans (6 oz. each) tomato paste
¼ cup water
¼ cup vinegar
1 tablespoon sugar
½ teaspoon onion powder
½ teaspoon salt
½ teaspoon pepper
dash cayenne pepper

Mix all ingredients and refrigerate in an airtight container. This mixture will not be as smooth and glossy as commercial ketchup, but is very similar in taste.

Dry Onion Soup Mix

¼ cup dried onion
1 tablespoon beef flavored bouillon
½ teaspoon onion powder
½ teaspoon salt
¼ teaspoon parsley flakes

Combine ingredients. Mixture can be substituted

for one envelope of Onion Soup Mix. Flavor will vary depending on brand of beef bouillon.

Mix Dry Onion Soup Mix with 16 oz. sour cream for tasty dip, or rub on beef roast before cooking.

White Gravy

1 cup powdered milk
3 cups water
¼ cup flour
½ teaspoon salt
¼ teaspoon pepper
2 tablespoons butter

Mix the powdered milk and water in a medium saucepan. Add flour, salt, and pepper and cook over medium heat stirring constantly until gravy is thickened and smooth. Add butter and stir until blended.

Tasty Tip: May substitute ¼ cup of pan drippings for ¼ cup water and omit butter.

Plain Yogurt

3¾ cups water
1½ cups powdered milk
¼ cup plain yogurt with active cultures

In a large saucepan, combine water and powdered milk over medium heat. Heat to 180°F, just below boiling point, stirring frequently. This will kill any competing bacteria. *Do not allow the milk to boil.* Remove milk from heat and let cool until lukewarm, about 110°F (not over 120°F). Add plain yogurt and stir gently to blend. You may have to stir for several minutes for the store-bought yogurt to completely dissolve. Pour into clean containers and let incubate in a warm spot (110°F) for 5 to 10 hours. See "Ways to Incubate" in Yogurt Tips. Chill.

Vanilla Yogurt

3¾ cups water
1½ cups powdered milk
1 envelope gelatin
¼ cup pure maple syrup (or sugar)
⅓ cup plain yogurt with active cultures
1 teaspoon vanilla

In a large saucepan combine water and powdered milk over medium heat. Heat to 180°F, just below boiling point, stirring frequently. This will kill any competing bacteria. *Do not allow the milk to boil.* Take out ¼ cup of milk and put in a separate bowl. Remove milk from heat and let cool until lukewarm, about 110°F (not

Yogurt Tips

Yogurt can be made from powdered, evaporated, skim, low fat, or whole milk.

Always use clean containers and utensils as the yogurt culture is affected by impurities.

Temperature is essential to get right when making yogurt, oherwise, the yogurt cultures will die. Puchase a good candy thermometer to take out the guess work.

When buying a commercial yogurt to use as a starter, always check the label for live active cultures. You must have live active cultures to make yogurt. Only use plain yogurt. You can use your new homemade yogurt as a starter for your next batch. However, the cultures weaken after several batches, so use a store-bought yogurt occasionally. You can also purchase a dry yogurt start like Yogourmet, typically found in the refrigerated section by the yogurt. Store in the refrigerator. Yogourmet has a refrigerated life of about one year.

Yogurt typically needs to incubate about 5 to 10 hours. Yogurt will be partially set and will continue to thicken as it is chilled. Chill at least three hours before using. Overnight chilling is preferable. The longer yogurt is incubated, the tarter it will taste. Homemade yogurt is not quite as smooth as commercially-made yogurt, which is normal.

The liquid that forms on yogurt is called whey. Drain it or stir it into the yogurt.

Ways to Incubate Your Yogurt

Yogurt Maker Method: I love the Salton Yogurt Maker because it makes one quart of yogurt in a single container similar to the size you would buy in the store. Most other yogurt makers use 6 to 8 small cups with about ½ cup to ¾ cup of yogurt in each, which can be a pain if you are using large quantities of yogurt. To use, follow the yogurt recipe and then pour milk mixture into yogurt maker container. Incubate in the yogurt machine according to directions. Perfect every time!

Oven Method: You can also incubate yogurt in your oven. Pour yogurt into clean jars. Preheat oven to 200°F. *Turn oven off* and then place jars inside oven. Close the door and *turn on* the light. Let yogurt incubate for 8 to 10 hours or overnight. If yogurt doesn't look set, take jars out of the oven, preheat to 200°F, *turn oven off*, and then return jars to the oven for another hour. Chill. Remember that yogurt will continue to thicken as it chills.

over 120°F). Add gelatin to the smaller portion of milk and completely dissolve. Add maple syrup, vanilla, and gelatin mixture to larger pan of milk and stir to combine. Add plain yogurt and stir gently to blend. You may have to stir for several minutes for the store-bought yogurt to completely dissolve. Pour yogurt into clean containers and let incubate in a warm spot (110°F) for 5 to 10 hours. See "Ways to Incubate" in Yogurt Tips. Chill.

Equivalent Measurements

1 gallon = 4 quarts = 8 pints = 16 cups

½ gallon = 2 quarts = 4 pints = 8 cups

¼ gallon = 1 quart = 2 pints = 4 cups

⅛ gallon = ½ quart = 1 pint = 2 cups

½ quart = 1 pint = 2 cups = 16 fluid oz

¼ quart = ½ pint = 1 cup = 8 fluid oz

1 cup = 8 fluid oz. = 16 tablespoons = 48 teaspoons

¾ cup = 6 fluid oz. = 12 tablespoons = 36 teaspoons

⅔ cup = 5 ⅓ fluid oz. = 10 tablespoons = 32 teaspoons

½ cup = 4 fluid oz. = 8 tablespoons = 24 teaspoons

⅓ cup = 2 ⅔ fluid oz. = 5 tablespoons = 16 teaspoons

¼ cup = 2 fluid oz. = 4 tablespoons = 12 teaspoons

⅛ cup = 1 fluid oz. = 2 tablespoons = 6 teaspoons

½ fluid oz. = 1 tablespoons = 3 teaspoons

Index

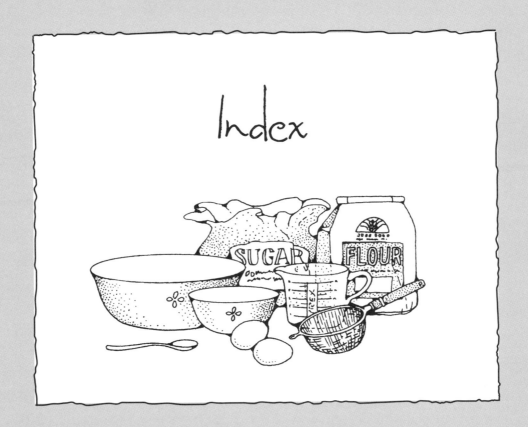

Index